SHOUT
IN THE
RIGHT
DIRECTION

How to Target Your Audience
and Amplify Your Voice on the Web

BY NICK ROSENER
& ERIC LEHNEN

Tech Nick Creative
722 S 10th St #2
Minneapolis, MN 55404
www.shoutintherightdirection.com

Ordering Information:
Quantity sales. Special discounts are available on quantity purchases by corporations, associations, and others. For details, contact the authors at the address above.

ISBN-10: 0-9847636-1-9
ISBN-13: 978-0-9847636-1-0
Library of Congress Control Number: 2014907631

To Britt, for putting up with me.
Nick

To Mom, Dad, and Melanie,
Thank you for the love and the support.
Eric

Table of Contents

1

Introduction

As a business owner, a marketer, or a brand manager, you're under pressure to keep your business going. We won't waste your time with hyperboles or magic tricks; we just want to share with you a practical and powerful way to think about your marketing. We want to help you *shout in the right direction.*

This book is about targeting your audience (also known as your target market) and amplifying your voice. Before connecting the two, you must identify your audience and your voice. It is a process, and you probably have at least one of them figured out. Even if you have them both figured out, we can help you perfect them. The goal we have for you by the end of the book is to hone your skills of identifying the target market that is most aligned with your business as well as the most effective channels to communicate with them.

At its core, "shouting" is all about making your message heard. Part of making your message heard is getting the right people to listen. Consumers are moving constantly. As they adapt to ever-evolving technology, their expectations about how brands and businesses interact with them change along with it. Think about what people spend their time doing. Working in the workshop? Working in the office? What about after that? The car? The grass? Even further? Cleaning? Showering? The dog? Don't forget sleep. As a marketer, you compete for attention span. And the different moments that people spend time on all the different activities of their busy lives, are marketing opportunities.

The book is divided into three parts: Plan, Tools, and Creative. The first part-Plan-is the backbone of all your marketing. We teach you how to write a marketing plan and turn it into an evolving company-building document. While we talk briefly about some of the tools used in this first part of the book, the second part-Tools-explains the various tools, such as social media, websites, and blogs that you have at your disposal. We explain specific uses for each and provide examples. Section three-Creative-is where everything comes together. In this section, we help you to incorporate your creative juices in your plan and tools.

Aristotle once said, "The whole is greater than the sum of its parts." Alone, a single part is not enough. You need the plan, the tools, and the creativity to get your message heard. By the end of the book, you will understand the importance of having a complete marketing plan. As long as you have all three components, even if it totals a single page long, you have a complete plan.

We get why many business leaders are too busy with other business functions or cannot risk trying something new. We get it. We understand, and more importantly, we have been in your shoes and have spoken with businesses of all sizes that were in the same situation. But they all got over this "hump" because they believed in change. More importantly, they believed they could do better.

How Can We Help You?

You bought this book for a reason. We're here to help. Are you intrigued by the idea that you can move your business beyond its current state? Maybe nothing is wrong with your marketing. Maybe you just want to learn how to improve your marketing strategies; you have tried a lot, you don't know what's next, or you have become curious about some unfamiliar strategies. Or perhaps you struggle with some underlying motivation or problem. Is your business stagnating? Do you need to grow? New competitor moved in? Whatever the reason, you are here now. Before doing anything to your marketing plan, the first thing you need to do is identify your "why." Once you have identified why you need to do something, it is time to get to work.

We want to help you reach the point where you are comfortable managing your marketing plan and your efforts help your business. The path to get there is not an easy one, but we will guide you. It is okay to get frustrated and feel that you have maxed yourself out. Any hard work will bring this out of all of us. We know this because we have been in your shoes and have helped others who went through the same process of improving their marketing. Marketing is difficult, especially if you are the only one at your business doing it. However, we've learned that it becomes easier when you dial in on what works for your situation—and when you see the benefits come to fruition!

What Is Shouting in the Right Direction?

Simply put, shouting in the right direction is about targeting your audience and amplifying your voice. Your ideal customers are your audience and your voice includes the many ways you communicate your value to them. This is Marketing 101. Why is it that many businesses feel that they are missing something, not hitting the goals that they set for themselves, or lack the time to set goals?

The root of the answers lies in the nature of owning a business. So many aspects of running a business take time away from marketing. Often times only an epiphany can instigate a major change in marketing.

To put in perspective, let's show you what it means to shout in the right direction:

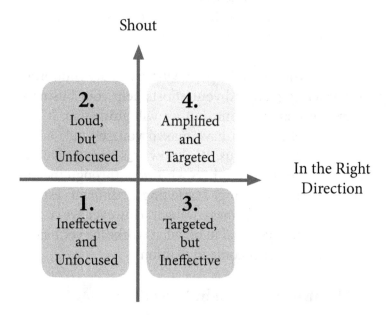

1. Ineffective and Unfocused
People in this category have just started marketing or are not getting enough traction. They seek to know and use the basics of digital marketing and ways to implement new strategies or improve current ones.

2. Loud, but Unfocused
These people definitely have a grasp on getting the right messages heard, but maybe they have not targeted it to the right audience. They want to learn how to discover and target their ideal audience.

3. Targeted, but Ineffective
These people understand who their audience is and know it extremely well. However, they miss potential customers because they are not engaging with the right tools. They want to improve the reach of their messages and utilize better tools.

4. Amplified and Targeted

These people have dialed into their audience and use the right messages, but want to revisit available tools and best practices to keep themselves updated and in shape.

Recognize yourself in any of these categories? Regardless of where you fit in, thinking about your business in terms of shouting in the right direction will help you focus on what is important to your business. As you go through this book, keep referring to the areas you want to know more about. This proactive approach will help you greatly, since we can only show you the way; you need to walk the path.

Perhaps you want to go beyond getting an overview of marketing strategies; you want to master them. Or, you want to focus on a specific area in digital marketing. Alternatively, you may be seeking inspiration. In any case, we go beyond introductory info and basic know-how; we demonstrate the benefits of following our suggestions with the stories of marketers using digital marketing in creative and effective ways.

While every author, consultant, and marketer says this, we have to say it, too: there is no fool-proof plan, formula, or one-size-fits-all strategy. Your strategy depends on your unique business situation, your current marketing, and your needs. There is good news, though! We've created a process that everyone can go through and get to where they want to be. That includes you.

Digital Marketing: The New Way to Communicate

With digital channels, almost endless opportunities exist for you and your target market. With social media, for instance, getting feedback from customers is wide open, whether you pay attention or not. People love to share and social media gives them places to praise (or complain about) products or services. The secret to using this to your business's advantage is knowing how to get people to praise you and how you can turn negatives into positives without spending all of your time doing it. It is surprisingly easy to do and exciting! We will cover this later on; we promise.

Online marketing brings another interesting advantage. Once your target market buys what you sell, send them to one of your online marketing platforms, such as a Facebook page, or keep them up-to-date with an e-mail newsletter. This will keep them updated about your offerings and provide an open invitation to come back to increase repeat business. You can't really do this with traditional marketing. Well, maybe you can do something similar with loyalty cards, but there is an app for that, too.

Kathy Davis is a perfect example of a smart businessperson focusing on marketing that makes sense for her. She started her career as an attorney working with small clients at an established law firm. As she moved up in the ranks, she was rewarded with the opportunity to work with larger clients. She was hoping that she would discover gratification working with these larger clients, but she never did. Kathy began to miss working with the smaller clients, which she had found much more enjoyable.

> *I kept thinking, well, sooner or later I'm going to just discover what's so wonderful about working with these bigger companies; sooner or later this is going to be fun for me. But I just saw companies making these decisions and doing things not based on 'Is this good for our company? Is this going to move us forward?' but more based on, 'Well, is this the safest option we can do. How can I basically cover my own ass the best?' This became ridiculous; I don't want to be this stumbling block for people who are just trying to do their jobs.*

The larger clients burned her out and she lost her passion when working with them. Among other reasons, including a tanking economy, she decided her leave her safe and stable attorney job to start her own firm focused on small business.

Before starting any digital marketing for her new firm, she used a few traditional channels such as running ads in local magazines and sponsoring events, but never found success. During this time, she really thought about why her traditional marketing wasn't working to the level she had hoped. It was clear that her target market—small businesses—weren't searching the Yellow Pages or local magazines when they needed legal guidance. They used Google.

> " I did some print marketing and some sponsorship of different things. Now, I really am only using social media and plain old face-to-face networking—and then Google AdWords has been amazing. "

Kathy saw her opportunity to go digital and adapted. She saw that prospects were actually using Google to find legal advice, but she had no idea initially —until she researched her audience. This motivated her to focus more of her marketing efforts on digital. However, she didn't dive in prematurely; she slowly added her digital tools as she became comfortable using them. After all, she is a busy attorney.

The first thing she worked on was her website. She worked with a designer so her site looked different from every other attorney's website. While it wasn't extraordinary, she said, it stood out from the rest. To keep visitors busy with great content, she incorporated a blog into her website. She had a brilliant idea to focus on blog posts that answered many of common questions she received from social media mentions or frequently searched questions on Google. With search engines favoring this kind of content, her page rank increased, making her site more likely to be found and more likely to convert anonymous visitors into leads. She found some of these commonly asked questions with the Google AdWords Keyword Planner (formerly Google AdWords Keyword Tool).

Aside from her website, she built a strong following on social media, specifically on Twitter and Facebook without devoting much time to it. While she is an attorney and holds a high level of professionalism, she is also personal. By adding this personal touch, she makes herself more interesting. She answered questions promptly and to the point, but she occasionally speaks her mind, just to remind everyone that she is human and not a boring attorney. Unfortunately, brands and businesses often neglect this important trait.

Professional Tweet Example:
@krautgrrl it's an agreement among owners that covers what happens if… various scenarios. I call it a business pre-nup/will. Vital.

Personal Tweet Example:
Okay, when is someone going to open some type of co-drinking bar in the available space downstairs of @CoCoMSP? #crowdfunding?

All it took for Kathy to rethink her marketing was the "Aha!" moment when she realized that her target market was Googling her! Kathy's marketing strategies were not complex nor were they expensive. But why did it work for her? She followed the same principles we discuss in *Shout in the Right Direction*. She discovered where her target market was: Google. She created strategies to get found: a blog, Google AdWords, a website, and social media. More importantly, she did something creative: She answers commonly asked questions, for free, and in a voice her audience can relate to!

She did not spam people with e-mails or mentions on social media; she allowed people to come to her with questions. Most importantly, she was real. Meaning, she was herself, a professional yet someone excited about her work and her clients.

By keeping her marketing plan simple and focused on the tools that mattered, Kathy built a self-sustaining business that she enjoys growing each day. As cliché as it sounds, it is true: She learned how to shout in the right direction. She didn't need a complex marketing plan, big budget, or savvy marketing director. She just needed to know what to do and how to do it. And she did it with passion.

This fundamental element is not found in textbooks; it is created in the real world. Kathy channeled her passion into what she enjoys most. In our experience, this way of "shouting" can have a dramatic effect, For Kathy, it made the difference between just enjoying her job and loving it. She told us, "This year, for the first time, I felt like, 'Oh, I can make a plan about how this is all going to work' and 'I can get it together.'

Different Approaches to Digital: Outbound and Inbound

Knowing the difference between inbound and outbound marketing will help you strategize and better identify the ideal strategies for your target market. Take Kathy's case, for instance. She focused more on traditional marketing (things like print ads, events, etc.) at first, but later found her target audience preferred digital channels. What is the significance of this? The answer lies in the difference between outbound and inbound marketing.

The difference between the two is simply the direction in which your leads travel; do you find leads (outbound marketing), or do leads find you (inbound marketing)? Outbound marketing focuses on sending messages to the target audience in hopes that those messages will cause that target audience to do something or think a certain way. The most common forms of outbound marketing are print, radio, and television. Inbound marketing focuses on creating pathways for your target audience to find you, such as pay-per-click (PPC) ads, e-mail, social media, blogs, and search engine optimization (SEO).

Another way to consider the difference is to think about the fundamental ways these two strategies work. Outbound marketing is often called "interruption marketing." Generally speaking, these strategies usually involve interrupting users with marketing messages while they are in the middle of something else. With inbound marketing, the audience takes the initiative to contact you. The mix of marketing methods you choose all depends on the needs of your brand or business. However, inbound marketing is becoming increasingly popular because of changing trends in how customers communicate. Instead of pushing messages and offers through outbound marketing, you can now focus on making your brand or business stand out and earn their interest, and that's powerful!

The marketing strategies you choose will, of course, depend on the type of business you have. For instance, if you sell large machinery to construction and manufacturing companies, it isn't likely that you will be using social media to connect with potential prospects.[1] A website, along

1   *Though this is changing rapidly, several industries that one would not traditionally consider to be "social savvy" are slowly becoming more open to digital marketers.*

with white papers or case studies detailing how your solutions can help your target market, can be a great part of a marketing strategy to back up and support the sales people you'll need for such large transactions.

In most situations, businesses and brands need strategies for reaching out to their target market *and* creating pathways for their target market to discover them. Think of it as playing baseball with your target market. You "pitch" your messages to your target market (outbound marketing) and after they hit the ball, you catch it (inbound marketing). It is a cycle of effort from both the target market and your brand or business.

With that in mind, we all know that the best plans often go awry. Customers don't always take the neat pathways we make for them. Think of the channels (tools) in your pathways as a create-your-own-story book by letting your customers decide what resonates best with them, and how they want to learn more about you. Here are a few examples of what your marketing pathways might look like:

Professional Services Company:
1. A potential customer searches for a relevant keyword that relates to one of the services the business offers.
2. The visitor clicks on the link generated by the search engine.
3. After briefly reading, the visitor downloads a free case study offered on the website.
4. Over the next month, the client receives an e-mail newsletter to get to know the business better.
5. A month later, after receiving five newsletters, they call to set up an appointment with the sales team.

Non-profit:
1. The non-profit sends out a direct mail campaign.
2. The recipient is interested to learn more and goes to the website provided.
3. The recipient watches a video on the website.
4. The recipient makes a donation.

E-commerce:
1. The visitor does a Google Search. A Google AdWords ad for the store sits above the search results.
2. The visitor clicks on the link from the AdWords ad, and it takes them to the website.
3. The visitor makes a purchase and in the process, shares it on Facebook.
4. The visitor's friends on Facebook see that their friend bought something from a company and end up making a purchase too.

As you shape and implement your marketing plan, begin by creating pathways one at a time and progress to add additional pathways as you master them. These additional pathways intertwine and lead prospects down different paths to your business, depending on their choices of content.

However, prospects are not always convinced right away. Outbound marketing seeks an action from the audience immediately, often a purchase or visit to a website. So what do you do to strengthen this request and encourage the action you want your audience to take? MORE ADS, OF COURSE! Well, maybe. You could get away with blasting more ads, since repetition is one element that aids in the success of promotion. However, the approach doesn't create value for your target audience, and people may get annoyed. Think of it as if you are fighting for their time on your terms.

Thankfully, this is where inbound marketing comes in. Inbound marketing eases your target market into a sale on their terms. It is less intrusive, less aggressive, and adds more value. Most importantly, your audience will get the chance to consume your content on their terms and at their convenience, not when you tell them to. When prospects want to get more information, they want it ASAP. Requiring prospects to jump over obstacles before they can access your content is a huge turn off. Businesses do this to turn their website into a lead generation tool. Use the curiosity of prospects to your advantage and turn your website into a salesperson. In general, creating a presence on multiple channels helps you customize these pathways to suit communication best for your customers.

This will help your target audience consume your content the way they want, where they are at their own pace, and it can help you organize a better sales process. The exact pathways you choose depend on your target audience. It follows that before you start building a pathway, you will want to research that market. We will talk about identifying the best channels for your target market in the "research" section.

When you engage in inbound marketing, the goal is to generate leads without direct interaction from your business. For instance, let's say you sell scented candles and one of your inbound marketing strategies is using Google AdWords with a teaser offer for a free pack of candles. A visitor will click on the ad and it will take them to a webpage where they fill out a form to order the free candles. All you did was create an inbound pathway for the new lead to discover you. Simple as that.

What's Your Type? Clients or Customers?

Do you sell products? Services? Both? Do you have clients or customers? What you sell and whom you sell to makes a difference in how you market your business.

Think about your business and how you earn revenue. Why is this important to know? The answer is simple: scale. As we all know, leading clients up to a sale requires giving them a lot of individual attention.

So which do you have: clients or customers? There are three key differences:
1. Relationship with the client/customer.
2. Revenue earned per client/customer.
3. Resources required making a sale.

Compare the products offered by a general department store and the services offered by attorneys. More people need shampoo than need an attorney. It is easier to choose a shampoo than choose an attorney. Fewer resources are required to choose a brand of shampoo than choose an attorney. And finally, department stores have less impact on the shampoo customers buy compared to the relationships clients have with their attorneys with buying legal services.

Spending time and money on clients and customers will show them they are important, and when they feel that they matter, they'll be more likely to purchase from you. When a new customer stops in your store or you follow up with a customer with an email or social media interaction after he or she makes a purchase, spending that extra five minutes can create a lasting impression. When it comes to important clients, giving them an extra five hours can help win that fifty thousand dollar contract you are working so hard to land.

Spending time and money to make clients and customers feel special is not a new strategy. Taking clients out to lunch or giving free products to customers is a common practice. Your challenge will be making your clients or customers feel important without spending more money or time per person than you can really afford.

When considering your available resources, the maximum number of clients or customers you are able to serve, and the goals you have, think about how your business operates best. Then figure out how you can take on more customers or clients with the same amount of resources. These types of considerations are exactly what you should use to shape your marketing plans.

The Why of Marketing

We all know that running a business is about much more than just "finding the right allocation of resources." Most of us don't find ourselves in business without first identifying a strong force driving us to do what we do.

In *The Matrix Reloaded*, a mob of Agent Smiths confronts Neo (Mr. Anderson) and explains its modus operandi:

These is no escaping reason, no denying purpose, because we both know without purpose, we would not exist. It is purpose that created us, purpose that connects us, purpose that pulls us, that guides us, that drives us. It is purpose that defines, purpose that binds us.

Just as Agent Smith explains, purpose defines why you do the things you do. The best marketing has PURPOSE. If what you are doing has no purpose, then there is no reason to continue. If you have no purpose, you have nothing to market. Having purpose unlocks creative ideas and relentless motivation. Purpose forms naturally and cannot be forced. In this book, we'll discuss about quite a bit about process. This process is nothing more than a set of directions to follow to set your marketing on a path to success. But just as a paint brush needs the hand of a talented artist to make a masterpiece, your business needs your spark of purpose to make the strategies covered in this book come to fruition. Digital marketing is a revolutionary field with massive potential waiting to be harnessed. It's ready and waiting for a person with purpose to put it to work.

The "why" is even more important for smaller businesses than it is for larger ones because they work harder to compete. This is exactly what we can see when a Walmart moves into a small town. The small businesses that are passionate about what they do find innovative ways to stay competitive and keep their customers. They have to use that passion to figure out how to compete against a giant amoral corporate blob that undercuts their prices at every turn. This is the power that we have as small companies. We succeed and grow by staying true to our purpose, and by creating businesses that customers and communities love.

All people who have jobs have duties, whether they like their job or not. However, some people want to make an impact, exceed goals, and build something they love. People who exist solely for paychecks won't likely be the next Sir Richard Branson, Guy Kawasaki, Seth Godin, Oprah

Winfrey, Michael Dell, or Mahatma Gandhi. You have to be passionate enough to sacrifice if you want to build something great.

Finding your business's why means justifying your business's existence: not just to you, but to your customers, your community, and to the world. It means answering these kinds of why questions:

- Why are you in business and why do you market for your business?
- Why do you provide your product/service instead of a different one?
- Why do you price your product/service the way you do?
- Why do you get up in the morning?

Your "why" is not just your value proposition or your competitive advantage. It is deeper than that. When you understand the why of your business, you create purpose, and purpose has meaning, and meaning gives your business life.

Finding your "why" isn't something to rush through nor is it something that is easy to do. The most basic "why" should describe fulfilling a need of your target audience. Think about that for a moment: businesses that can define their "why" don't just create shareholder value, they create customer value. They don't just create profits, they create experiences. They don't just build products, they build lives. When your why is clear, everything just works. Once you have your why, you can begin to shout in the right direction.

So let's start now.

Part I – Building a Plan

2

The Need

If you are a business owner, you have bills to pay, people to serve, things to fix, supplies to order, and people to manage, all the while trying to fit sleep in there, too. The last thing that you have time for is marketing. Whatever stage your business is in, marketing is a function that costs lots of time if not money (and most of the time, it costs both). We want to shift your perspective about marketing from "marketing costs money" to "marketing makes money." This, we've found, is one of the key mindsets that will help you shout in the right direction. Most businesses understand the importance of marketing, but have difficulty deciding where to invest their time. Or they run into the trap of only focusing on business operations and forgetting marketing.

Sound familiar? Can you relate to this situation? Have you worked hard to create something only to watch it fall apart in the execution? This is why we start this book with building a plan. Before we arm you with the tools you need to accomplish your goals, set the direction. Right out of the gate, most businesses start their marketing plan by building a Facebook page and hoping for the best. Without a cohesive direction that aligns the marketing actives with business goals, it is unlikely that the outcome will turn out the way you're hoping. This is why we plan. The plan you will create will encompass research, planning, execution, and measuring your marketing goals. This is a great place to start.

What Is in a Marketing Plan?

Plans, whether they are marketing plans, business plans, or communication plans, all work in a similar way. A plan is simply a document that lists all the actions you will take to achieve a goal. But creating a plan is only a single step in the marketing plan process.

The strategic planning cycle consists of five major phases:

- Research (gathering any helpful information)
- Planning (the who, what, when, where, how, and why)
- Execution (launching the plan)
- Measurement (evaluating success)
- Repeat (what to do next time)

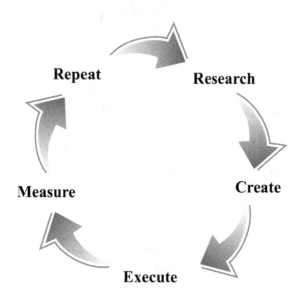

As you begin the planning cycle, the research phase helps you gather information that assists with creating a plan. Once you've collected and analyzed the relevant information, the planning phase involves organizing all your goals and strategies into a single document that communicates the plan and builds accountability. Once built, you execute the marketing plan (and yes, there is further planning behind the execution). Finally, the measure section explains how you will measure the success of the plan. After your first plan, you start the process all over again by continuing what worked and cutting what didn't. Hooray!

Marketing plans are short-term steps toward your business's long-term goals, and to stop after one marketing plan holds your business back from building on the previous plan's success. You can tell yourself that you will do some of the same things from the marketing plan again, but investing your time and resources to organize your actions keeps you accountable.

Before you dive in to creating your plan, you will want to identify whom you are going to be reaching. And that, our friend, is where the fun of segment, target, position (STP) strategy begins.

3

Segment, Target, Position (STP) Strategy

There are seven billion people in this world. Can you imagine trying to sell to seven billion people? So where do you start? Odds are there may be some people in the world who will never buy from you. Even worse, some of the people that will buy from you may turn out to be crappy clients. If your marketing plan allocates any time or energy to marketing to these people, those resources are wasted. It sounds simple, but every business we've worked with has had some program or strategy that targets people who can't buy. It's a serious issue. So, let's assume that we want to focus on customers who can buy from us. How might we go about that?

What if you had an infinite budget to do all of the marketing you wanted? Most likely, you would market to everyone you could. Now, what if that "unlimited" budget were cut in half? Or to a fourth? Or tenth? Or one hundredth? Clearly, your business cannot afford the infinitely large marketing budget and you'll need to choose the best people to market to. This is the reality for every business because the infinite budget does not exist. How do you maximize your marketing while staying within your business constraints? This is where STP, or Segment Target Position strategy, comes in. That is to say, you must understand who to market to, as well as why and how to get your messages to stick with who you market to.

By only focusing on the people that matter, you have a better chance of success. While *that* may be obvious, it's not so obvious how to narrow down the vast sea of consumers to this pool of people. The segment, target, position process will help you map out the people that resonate best with your business.

SEGMENT: Identify Groups of People

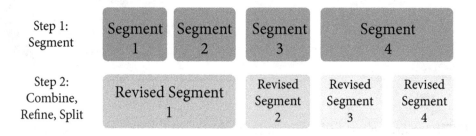

Segmenting is the process placing your potential customers into groups around common characteristics. For business-to-consumer (B2C; those who sell to individuals) companies, example traits include: location, age, income, education, interests, morals, technical understanding, and buying styles. For business-to-business (B2B; those who sell to businesses) companies, use industry, location, number of employees, and revenue.

Keep in mind that you may have more than one target market, and each may be entirely different from another. Since they can be different, you will need separate messages to market to each

How to identify great segments:

1. Brainstorm all potential groups of people to whom you might market.

2. Refine your segments by combining similar groups and splitting groups that aren't uniform or are too large.

3. Refine further by giving more details about the specific type of person in the segment. Develop a policy on who is and isn't a member of this segment. Identify examples of ideal representatives of the segment to bring a face to the group.

4. Perform a reality check. Will these segments work for your business? The way you segment your customers will have a large impact on upcoming steps. Make sure they're workable for your business.

What useful segments look like:

Continue to refine your segments until you're comfortable that what you've chosen fits your business well. By the time you're done, your chosen segments should have the following qualities:

- Uniformity: When you identify a segment, you should be able to communicate to everyone in that segment the same way They should have a similar set of problems, and your business should have a relatively standard offering for everyone in the segment.

- Specificity: Each segment should be specific enough that you can clearly identify people who are members based on a standard set of criteria.

- Identifiability: When you meet a new potential prospect, you should be able to tell which of your segments they fit, based on publically or conversationally available factors.

- Mutual exclusivity: Any prospect you meet should fit neatly into only one segment.

- Appropriate number: A segmenting strategy breaks down when you create too many or too few segments. Having too few segments doesn't allow for you to adequately customize messaging and positioning for each segment. Having too many segments forces you to dedicate too many resources to creating individualized communications for each segment. Balance is key and the optimum number of segments depends on your company and marketing budget.

Developing a solid segmentation plan is one of the cornerstones of developing your STP strategy, and your whole marketing strategy. Once you feel that you've identified the relevant segments for your company, proceed to the next step to decide which of your segments you're going to focus on.

TARGET: Select a Market to Focus on

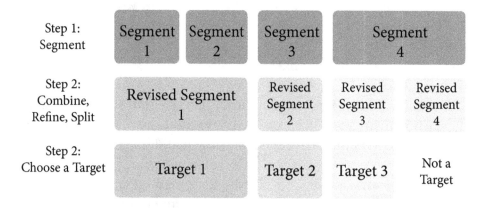

Targeting is the process of choosing which of your segments you would like to focus on. One of the largest challenges small businesses face is choosing too many segments to target. As entrepreneurs, we're idea people. We see opportunities that other people don't. Because of this, we're prone to thinking that our products or services can help everyone in the world! This is great, until we realize that we've just committed ourselves to marketing to everyone in the world. To top it all off, we have a marketing staff of zero and a marketing budget nearly the same.

Choosing the right target market is not an easy decision because you are making a commitment to focus your marketing on this group of people. To put targeting into perspective, let's perform a short thought experiment. Pretend for a moment that you're going to hire a salesperson. To whom should your salesperson sell? Naturally, we would want them to focus on the best segments and ignore the others. You want them to focus on a specific target market because their time will be devoted to building their network and assimilating within that market. This focus translates into an efficient use of resources.

Criteria for choosing the right target market:

1. What are the differences between the markets?
2. How difficult is it to market to each?
3. How much can you make from the market?
4. How well do your current product and service offerings resonate with the target?
5. Do you need to create a new product or service for the market?

One caveat: there are a few dark sides to this intense focus. If you choose to focus all your marketing efforts on one area, you can multiply your success if you make the right choice. Unfortunately, you also lose the safety net that you would have had if you spread your segments out. Sometimes you'll choose a bad egg. Finding your target-market sweet spot takes a little trial, error, and creativity. Thankfully, we will help you with this throughout the book. Additionally, each target market is different and requires a certain amount of time, resources, and effort to be successful in reaching it. Having more than one market can dilute your marketing efforts and create more work for you. When you decide to add target markets, you will likely need more time and resources. For most businesses, these are limited.

At the end of the day, we have to start somewhere. All you can do is choose the best targets that you can based on the information you have available.

POSITION: Position Yourself to Best Reach Them

	Target 1	Target 2	Target 3
Product 1	x	Benefit 1	Benefit 2
Product 2	Benefit 3	x	x
Product 3	x	Benefit 4	x

X = Not Targeted

Positioning is the process of designing messages that perfectly matches your products or services with the people you want to sell to. The goal of STP is to better utilize your time, resources, and efforts by focusing on the best target market(s). How does this happen? Since you'll customize your message individually for each of your chosen target segments, the messages and methods you'll have will have a better chance of success than if you didn't target effectively. Think of it this way: Would you market to senior citizens and teenagers the same way? Likely not. Without positioning your messages to the right market, your messages will lose relevance. At the same time, marketing to everyone simultaneously isn't any better. Going down that route leaves you with a bland message that isn't *really* relevant to anyone. When you plan ahead and choose your market carefully, you'll be able to craft a message that really sings

Part of the positioning process is aligning your messages to your market, but it also involves aligning your market to your products and services. Consider how much adjusting your market impacts your products or services. If you make a *drastic* change to the groups you market to, it will certainly affect your products or services. If there is a slight mismatch of your offering with your market, you'll need to make refinements to the market and your products or services.

Until now, when we have been talking about segments, we have been referring to segmenting *customers* into groups. This type of segmentation is called *vertical segmentation*. On the positioning chart above, you can see that the vertical segments (our target verticals) each head up one of the vertical columns. When you are planning your positioning messages, there's another useful way to look at your segments: *horizontal segmentation*. Where vertical segments refer to categories of customers, horizontal segments refer to categories of products and services.

To analyze this, draw a grid of what you are selling and who buys it. We included a simple example to explain this. This business uses a multi-targeted approach: three offerings and three target audiences. Since a target market is a group of people who share similarities, they are significantly different. Having three target audiences does not mean that the business won't sell to people who do not fall into one of the target markets. It simply means the business will focus on the markets that matter to it by creating a marketing plan for each. This example will require three separate marketing plans. Each plan can be identical in terms of goals and strategies, as long as the messages are tailored to the market. The point of each plan is to create the most relevance.

STP In Action: LASER Classroom

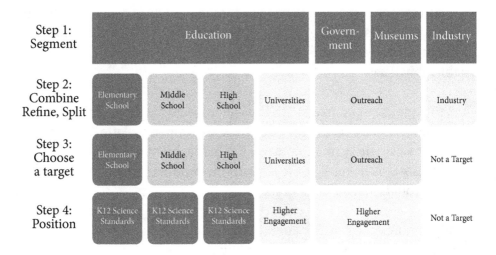

LASER Classroom manufactures educational products for education, government, museums, and industry to help educators teach topics related to light and lasers. The owner, Colette DeHarpporte, had recently repurposed her years of experience as a laser pointer distributor to create a series of products focused on the education market. While one would think that simply shifting focus to education would be enough, Colette found herself pulled in several different directions. She needed to clarify her marketing focus by better understanding her best customers.

Before going through the STP process, Colette identified four main segments: education, government, museums, and industry. However, what seemed to be a sensible way to group customers began to break down when she started getting specific about client needs and messaging.

For example, in the education segment she was marketing to elementary schools, middle schools, high schools, and universities. Not only did each of those markets have different education needs, but the decision makers even used different language to describe the product. Elementary teachers tended to ask about "light" and "lasers," with high school and university folks talking about "optics" and "photonics." It's not easy to market to a customer segment if you can't even agree on the words to use. It was time to make some updates to the segments.

Colette's first task was splitting up the educational market into elementary school teachers, middle school teachers, high school teachers, and university professors. Right away, this improved her business's ability to communicate by being able to customize language and packages to the right submarket.

Just the opposite occurred with the government and museum segments. Because their uses of the product were so similar, Colette consolidated them into a single segment: outreach. This segment centered on the central purpose of using LASER Classroom products to engage with students through outreach programs.

Lastly, a quick look at the contacts Colette had made in the industrial market showed that those leads hardly ever converted to sales, despite the fact that she had made significant progress in developing industry credibility and trade publication press. As it turned out, this was one of those cases where even though the owner had put lots of effort into developing a certain segment, the sales just didn't come as expected. In the interest of consolidating resources where they could be most useful, Colette cut the industry segment altogether.

From the beginning of the process, starting with four segments that didn't serve the business as well as they could, LASER Classroom was able to redefine how the company looked at its market to create segments that were more closely aligned with business goals.

Like most businesses, LASER Classroom has a few different types of products. As you might imagine, not all of the products align with every segment. The company's flagship product, LASER Blox™ is their main offering. As such, it has the broadest applicability; it is relevant to all but one of their target markets. Since lasers can be dangerous if shined into eyes, many elementary schools prefer to use safer alternatives when teaching topics about light. For this purpose, LASER Classroom offers Light Blox, a comparable product that uses lights instead of lasers to teach optics topics to younger children without the safety concerns. In addition to the education products, LASER Classroom also offers high-end research lasers. These more expensive lasers are only for university professors who run research labs; this represents yet another value proposition and product / target match.

Segments / Value Offering	Elementary School Teachers	Middle School Teachers	High School Teachers	Universities Professor and Lab Demonstrators	Outreach
LASER Blox (TM)	X	Meet Science Standards	Meet Science Standards	Better Lecture Demonstrations and Labs	Better Engagment
Light Blox	Safe for Young Children	Safe for Young Children	X	X	X
Research Lasers	X	X	X	United States Distributor	X

X = Not Targeted

After Colette refocused her efforts on the right target markets, she aligned them with her products. She consolidated all of her efforts for the seven product/market matches into a single marketing plan.

Once she developed an STP plan for the business, the rest of the marketing came together more easily. The new website developed with the plan in mind was laser-focused (pun intended) on exactly the audiences that she wanted to reach. The blog, social media, and e-mail strategy also became more tailored to the targets she cared about, and no one else.

The process that LASER Classroom went through to identify their Segments, Targets, and Positioning is similar to what many businesses go through when they want to improve their marketing. As you go through this process with your own company, remember that you're not alone. You're making a tangible investment in improving the clarity and focus of your company. When your strategy works, opportunity follows.

4

Research: What Is Research?

Everyone knows the saying "If it ain't broke, don't fix it." However, without adapting to our ever-changing world, any status-quo business is doomed to fail. Thomas Friedman explains this in his book *The World is Flat:* In order to stay competitive, people need to have the best tools and skills.[1] Being competitive isn't without its risk, either. It requires an investment of resources, sometimes without a return on that investment.

A research plan is triggered by a problem or a need. Growing competitors, shifting markets, lost consumers, and shrinking revenues all can initiate momentum to create a marketing plan. Businesses often recognize such reasons after realizing, "Oh wow; I didn't know that was going on," or "We need to fix that ASAP," and sometimes, "Let's try something different." These then becomes goal(s) for a marketing plan. If you have a problem or a need, but are unable to narrow it down to a goal, or don't have a problem at all, research will be your best friend to discover your goal. If you have a problem to fix or a goal to reach, you can immediately

1   Friedman, Thomas L. *The World Is Flat: A Brief History of the Twenty-First Centu-ry.* New York: Picador/Farrar, Straus and Giroux, 2007.

start the marketing plan by researching what you need to fix the problem or achieve your goal.

Research on your market, business, and competitors is the backbone of your marketing plan because it gives justification for your actions:

> *There is a wide range of pricing for my service area in the marketplace. Where do I fit?*

> *Many new companies are starting up in my area that compete with me. How can I differentiate myself?*

> *My ideal customers feel like they're evolving. How, exactly are they different?*

If you want to push your business to be more profitable, stable, and competitive—and if you want to shout in the right direction and capture the attention of the right target market—you need research to guide your marketing plan. However, it's hard to know how much research you actually need. The best indicator is answering this question at every stage: With the research I've done so far, can I create a plan that will meet my goals? The more difficult the goals, the more you should research. But that doesn't mean taking the easy route and going for the low-hanging fruit.

We encourage you to regard research not as an obstacle, but as an opportunity to learn what is happening around your business and to justify actions outlined in your marketing plan. So don't dread it or let it intimidate you. There are many ways to research, and you can gather much information quite easily. You may even find that research is actually quite interesting and helpful for your business. With a little creativity and direction, you will find information to create a solid marketing plan.

In the upcoming sections of research, we will show how to determine your goals, identify what you need to research to meet your goals, and research them. The research we will talk about is nothing fancy; it doesn't involve people in lab coats with clipboards, peering through a one-way mirror at people like lab rats. What we'll recommend will be easy to understand and well worth your time. We're not talking Ph.D.-level statistics, here. We're about common-sense ways for you to gather key insights about your company, so you don't start your marketing plan flying blind.

Step One: Find Your Marketing Plan Goal

Starting your marketing plan with research gives you a blank slate to develop your goals and actions. Before researching anything, your business needs a goal to focus on. Research only makes sense when directed at something that helps you solve a business problem. When setting your goals, think of your most pressing business goals and follow from there. Effective research will help you clarify the best approach for meeting your goals.

Let's say, for example, that your company's profit is lower than you would like. If this is the case, you may have chosen a business goal to increase profit in the following quarter. As you are likely aware, there are several different ways to raise profit:

- Get more new customers
- Increase profit margin
- Increase repeat business
- The list goes on . . .

You might set a research goal help you find out which of these strategies for raising profit will be most effective in helping you meet your business goal. If your business has a clear problem to fix or a need, this part is easy. From your problem or need, derive a goal. For example, if your revenue is lagging, an effective goal would be to increase revenue by a certain percentage. Or if your marketing isn't bringing in enough new customers, set a goal to add a measurable amount of new customers. Keep in mind that a goal should be both to the point and measurable.

By tying your marketing plan to a goal derived from a business problem or need, your marketing efforts will become objective orientated and not an exercise in "whatever happens, happens." Marketing plans without a measurable goal turn into a never-ending plan, or worse, a plan that you eventually scrap.

If you do not have a goal yet, take the opportunity to learn what your business can do better by researching your business, target market, and competitors. Then, use that information to define what you would like to improve on or how fix a problem that you came across in your research. In the upcoming section, we will explain what to research. The methods we describe also will help you identify a goal if you do not have one yet.

Step Two: Define What You Need to Research

We cannot stress how important good research is for building a marketing plan. Research provides you with valuable insight on all the "who, what, where, when, how, and why" that impact your business. The better you can define these portions of your marketing plan, the more refined strategies you will develop and the better chance you'll have of reaching your goals.

This research section will point you toward areas for research that you probably didn't know about and show you how easy it is to gather information in those areas.

Without realizing it, when you create a marketing plan you base it on a set of assumptions. Even the simplest goals have several assumptions that must be satisfied for the goal to be completed successfully. Take, for example, the following goal:

Sell $5000 of computer equipment in the 4th quarter.

In order for this to happen, several things must also happen, including:
- Customers must want computer equipment.
- Customers must be willing to pay a price where you can make a profit.
- Your computer equipment must have a competitive set of features.

- Many more assumptions that will affect your success in achieving the sales goal.

How do you know if these assumptions are reasonable? Research.

We see research goals as a collection of unanswered questions that test our assumptions. Write a list of questions that will help you understand more about your business, target market, and competitors. Make them specific and open-ended to gather more definitive information such as: Which of your marketing efforts creates more revenue (and why)? How much does the average customer spend at my store (and why)? What are my best-selling products/services (and why)? By asking these questions and providing answers, you will derive information that will tell you what to do to meet your goal. Since all research efforts will revolve around how to meet your goal, you will find that as you ask and answer these types of questions, new ones will arise and help you develop clearer methods of meeting your goals.

At the basic level, research is a process for you to answer and be confident with these questions:

Who
- Who is my target audience?
- Who are my competitors and what are their marketing strategies?

What
- What am I good at or do better than my competitors?
- What can I improve on or what are my disadvantages?

Where
- Where are your marketing actions taking place?
- Does my business need to be online, offline, or both?

When
- When should I start my marketing plan?
- When does each of my actions start?

How
- How am I going to communicate with my target market?
- How much time do I have to create and execute the marketing plan?

- How much of my resources do I devote to my marketing plan (time, effort, money, employees)?

Why
- Why should my target market buy my product/service rather than my competitors'?
- Why am I doing this marketing plan (what's my goal)?

If you can answer these questions, you will fulfill most of the research you'll need for starting a marketing plan. Use our questions as a springboard to create other questions to answer. Remember: start small. The worst thing that you can do is spend all of your time researching but never create any action from it. As the saying goes, "done is better than perfect."

Using Your Website, Blog, Or Social Media For Research

You may already be sitting on a wealth of information that can help you reach your marketing goals. If you already have a website, a blog, or a few social media tools in place, use the following sections to help develop research ideas to help your marketing plan. If you do not have any of these tools, or if you're starting from scratch, you can skip this section. But if you have any website or blog data already, you can use that data to gain valuable insights into customer behavior to support your marketing plan. Remember, this section isn't about how to use these tools to do marketing, it's about how to use the tools to do research that supports your marketing plan. We'll cover tools in Part II.

Your Website
When you tap a good oil well, monitor it closely to quickly adapt when production slows or the well runs dry. Keeping tabs on customers has the long-term benefit of letting you analyze how well your marketing is working. By monitoring trends, you can understand what works and how to fix problems before they start. Here are a few common questions to ask yourself about your website:
- Does my website do what it is intended to do?
- On what pages do people enter my website and why?

- On what pages do people exit my website and why?
- What pages have the most traffic and why?
- How often do people return?
- Where is the geography of my web traffic? What does it tell me?

If you do not have a website yet:
- Do your competitors have a website?
- What are your competitors' websites like? Do they have an online store, promote their store or talk about their advantages?
- If you had a website, what would you like it to do?

Blogs

Blogs are an easy way to stay up to date with your target market and competitors. Spend some time searching for information via search engines by narrowing your search to blogs. Both Yahoo! and Google allow you to narrow searches to blogs. Why are blogs important for your business? There are millions of blogs out there—literally! Many of them range in influence and reach. In terms of gathering information, many of these blogs have the potential to reference something about your business, customers, or market. For instance, if you are in the fashion industry, it would be helpful for you to know what fashion trends are popular in your area. Blogs can give you the answer. Another great resource is Technorati.com. Technorati is the Google for blogs, allowing you to search for any type of blog.

If you have a blog, here are a few common questions to ask yourself:
- What is my blog's purpose?
- How often do I post?
- Who is the audience of the blog?
- How many people subscribe my blog?
- How many comments do I receive?
- Is my blog shared often?

If you don't have a blog, evaluate your target audience's or competitor's blogs:
- If you can find a blog from your target audience or a competitor, identify the topics they cover.

- What do the blog posts tell you? Can you identify anything new you didn't know about them already?
- Do the blog posts get shared on social media or other blogs?
- Is there information that will help your marketing plan?

Social Media

With the many tools at your disposal such as Twitter, Facebook, YouTube, Instagram, LinkedIn, Pinterest, and Google+, how the heck do you keep track of it all? It presents an opportunity to engage with those people and learn how you might grow your business. There are many channels to monitor and these are great ways to find out what people think of your business. The overall goal is evaluate your business, competitors, and target market online by searching.

Tools like Socialmention.com allow you to search for keywords and give insight on what people are saying on these sites. Or if you find that a lot of your business comes from social media, consider purchasing software to help you manage this.

If you use social media, answer these questions:
- What does my target audience like to talk about?
- What does my target market say about my business and my competitors?
- Are my top customers on social media?
- What do I use these social media tools for?

If you do not use social media:
- Is my target audience on social media? My competitors?
- What do they say?
- What common themes of conversation do you see?

Evaluating your current marketing will add perspective to the research you should focus on. Use what is working and what isn't to steer what to do in your marketing plan. If you know that some strategies do wonderfully, use them as a cornerstone. If some of your strategies are just, well, bad, then explain why and don't use them in the plan.

Step Three: Dive In

Now that you have a list of questions, let's find the answers one at a time. But how? Reading industry websites or blogs, keeping up with news, asking your customers questions, comparing competitors websites and social media, doing social media searches, analyzing your web traffic, and consulting experts are all different ways to collect the information you need and do your research. Much of this may come from your own exploration; all you need to do is synthesize that research into actionable information.

Remember Kathy Davis? She left a large law firm to start her own firm that focused on small businesses and start-ups. She understood the needs of her target market well, but what she didn't know well was how to sell herself. Kathy took to social media and asked her followers what they wanted. She found that many clients didn't feel comfortable paying an entire legal bill all at once. She also uncovered that businesses have different needs at different stages of the business. So she created all-in-one packages.

These packages are streamlined to save time both for clients and Kathy, which ultimately saves the client even more money. One package is called "Let's get it started" and it includes all registrations, business agreements, and other documents to start a business. She also set up a twelve-month payment plan, making it easier for clients to pay. All she had to do was ask her clients what they needed so she could meet those needs directly. This kind of questioning is definitely part of shouting in the right direction.

Since she relies heavily on people searching online for her, it was very important for her to improve her company's visibility on search engines. After doing a little research with Google AdWords Keyword Planner and Google Analytics, she discovered that many prospective clients type common legal questions in search engines. To take advantage of this, she answered these frequently-asked questions on her website, making her site more likely to be in the top ten search results when people searched for answers to those questions.

When people think of marketing research, they think of traditional methods: focus groups, surveys, interviews, personal observations, and statistical analysis. For digital marketing, the techniques are similar. For example, personal observation traditionally involves marketers watching people browse through a store. On the digital side, marketers observe consumers browsing on a website. Both have the same intended purpose of improving the website or store—it is just done a little differently.

Digital marketing creates a new playing field for small businesses because it offers a twist on traditional methods. Let's say your business is trying to market a new product and you want to get feedback before you release it. Reach out to your customers directly through social media by giving free samples. Asking for feedback online is free and has the added benefit of generating word of mouth. If you want to gain valuable feedback and promote your product/service at the same time, try doing some research about it online.

How DipYourCar.com Used Research to Rock the Auto Modification Market

DipYourCar.com provides us with a great example of *how* to quickly build a simple but powerful marketing plan on just enough research. The story of DipYourCar doesn't start with how it exploded in growth in just two years. It starts the same as many great inventions: by accident.

Fonzie (he just goes by Fonzie), president of DipYourCar, has always been a passionate car guy and never kept his cars unmodified. In other words, he loved to tinker with the car's performance and cosmetics. Four years ago, curiosity got the best of him and he wanted to experiment with the color of his car's wheels. He grabbed a can of black spray paint and began to spray the paint on one of his wheels. After leaving the wheel to dry for a day, he ran his hands around the edge of the wheel to inspect the finish. He noticed that if he tried hard enough, he could peel the paint off. His jaw dropped and thought to himself, "Normal paint is not supposed to come off like this." Realizing that he used Plasti Dip and not typical spray paint, he said aloud to himself, "If this does what I think it's doing, this could be huge."

For car guys who love to customize the color of anything on cars, Plasti Dip is a perfect product. It allows users to spray nearly any surface and peel off the paint whenever they want to; it leaves no residue but will last for years. Typically, customizing cars, especially the color of the body and wheels, can get expensive and is often permanent. Plasti Dip acts like paint, but comes off when you want it to.

Fonzie came up with the idea to market Plasti Dip for automotive purposes, but before running with this idea and creating a marketing plan, he had to do product research.

"I wanted to make sure that, if this is something I am going to run with, I can't get surprised by anything that I don't want to be surprised by. I am not the type of guy to make a statement before I know it's a statement, and I don't like regretting things, let alone regretting saying things."

He spent roughly four thousand dollars in the next six months testing different products on every surface and under any condition so he could stand behind the product 100 percent.

After testing the product and winning his own seal of approval, Fonzie contacted Plasti Dip and asked them if the company currently marketed their products for automotive uses. He spoke with the sales manager and discovered that they had no intentions of targeting their products in the automotive market. Fireworks went off in his head. He spent the next week building DipYourCar and registered the business. Fonzie called Plasti Dip and created a distribution contract. This was all done while working a nine-to-five job.

DipYourCar was in a unique position when Fonzie first started it. Simply put, DipYouCar.com is a distributor of Plasti Dip products. Customers can buy Plasti Dip at most hardware stores, but it has never been targeted for automotive uses and no other distributors were doing what Fonzie decided to do. However, a competitor could easily catch or pass him, so he had to get his marketing plan implemented as fast as possible.

While Fonzie's new company didn't have any direct competitors yet, there were plenty of indirect competitors that Fonzie knew he had to understand. He had to be mindful of the current indirect competitors (vinyl wrapping and professional painters) and future competitors. He drafted the guts of his marketing plan in a room he had transformed into a giant white board. He described his process as, "Complete mayhem. You just couldn't make sense of it." Like any basic marketing plan, he needed to cover the four Ps: price, place, product, and promotion. In the mayhem of mind maps and puked-out ideas, he covered everything needed to launch his business quickly.

Place

The DipYourCar e-commerce website enabled the company to sell quickly and efficiently to DIYers, and to sell internationally.

However, Fonzie knew that some people would want to customize their cars with Plasti Dip, but wouldn't want to do it themselves. So Fonzie created the "Authorized DipYourCar Installer" network of local install-ers. Customers use the website to search for local installers in their ar-eas who will "dip" their cars professionally. This creates a win-win-win situation, since non-DIYers can find professionals to work on their cars, local installers promote their businesses on the DipYourCar website and receive product discounts, and DipYourCar gains another channel to sell products—increasing sales volume and minimizing installers pur-chasing Plasti Dip through other sources.

Fonzie created another win-win opportunity for those who want to be resellers of Plasti Dip through DipYourCar. A reseller just needs to regis-ter a business and create a website. The reseller handles promotion while DipYourCar handles distribution and logistics, so the reseller never has to manage inventory.

Price

Since DipYourCar owns most of the marketing for the automotive ap-plication of Plasti Dip, Fonzie does not have to worry too much about price. Price isn't an important factor of DipYourCar's marketing, either, because Plasti Dip presets price through a distribution contract. Aside from selling Plasti Dip, DipYourCar also professionally paints custom-ers' cars locally. The price to paint a customer car by a professional in-staller or DipYourCar varies according to the application.

Product

The primary product DipYourCar offers is obviously Plasti Dip. When the company first started, Plasti Dip only had a few products available. After DipYourCar began to establish itself, Plasti Dip noticed the effect of DipYourCar on product demand. This enabled Fonzie to leverage his brand to demand new products to meet the needs of his market. Over time, DipYourCar came to offer new products created by Plasti Dip as well as products that DipYourCar created as customer needs arose.

Promotion

Fonzie certainly possessed one key advantage: he was his own demographic. This made creating his marketing plan easier, because since he knew how *he* responded to certain marketing, he could accurately predict how others like him would respond.

Fonzie spent most of his time figuring out the promotion component of his marketing plan. He could enjoy this luxury because he had most of the price, place, and product issues figured out when he started. Since he was the first distributor to market directly to the automotive market, he had to start quickly. Coming from the aftermarket car world, he knew that online car forums are great places to connect with potential customers. He joined a popular online car forum to promote his product by sharing his knowledge of and experience in using Plasti Dip.

When determining how to best promote DipYourCar, Fonzie quickly focused on YouTube as potentially the most important tool available to him. And he was right. YouTube propelled his company to success. What made his videos go viral on YouTube was not a sales pitch or a great deal, but rather his ability to intrigue viewers by creating tutorials about different applications, colors, ideas, and techniques. This continues to be his flagship marketing tactic.

Each tool that DipYourCar uses has a specific purpose driven by customers. Fonzie was very particular in how he presented himself and DipYourCar and he adopted a very simple concept: run this entire company exactly the way I wish it would be run if I were a customer. For example, he presents himself as an ordinary guy in his tutorial videos on YouTube. This helps customers relate to him and makes customers feel inspired to learn more about using the product. In other words, he wanted to tell to his customers, "If I can do it, so can you." This strategy touches every tool he uses. He will never send out anything that contains sales language or cheesy pitches. It was important for him personally, but also a critical strategy in the business to be professional, relatable, and empathetic.

Additionally, to stay accountable and drive growth, Fonzie tied a specific goal to each tool. He believed firmly that in order to be successful, he had to set goals for each tool.

Success was measured in a comical way: Each time Fonzie would set a goal for his marketing, he would hit it early. This is proof that paying constant attention to your marketing tools pays off. Here is a great example: When DipYourCar first started using Google AdWords Fonzie experimented to gain a benchmark of what worked and what didn't. He found that text ads worked best in converting traffic into customers, and that image ads worked best in informing traffic about Plasti Dip. Upon realizing this, he felt that his marketing budget would be better used if he went with text ads, because they are the ones that create sales. Coming to this conclusion required constant attention while he was experimenting, but it helped sales significantly.

To help him understand what tools were working best for DipYourCar, Fonzie created a system to track everything. Now, each week his team creates a research report of all the tools they use. Here are some examples of what they try to ascertain from this report:

- How many people interacted with us on social media?
- What impact did this interaction have?
- How well did a specific Facebook post help the company?
- What created the most sales and why?
- Why are some people buying and others leaving their online shopping cart empty?
- When people click on certain promotions, how many people buy?

Fonzie was able to create a simple and easy-to-follow system to give DipYourCar a constant readout of how their marketing was performing. This gives the company a great platform to create their marketing plan with easy access to relevant information.

5

Plan: Get It on Paper

Finally, you have arrived at the big step: creating your plan! This is where your creative juices will flow. To put it plainly, your plan needs to answer six main questions:

- What is the goal?
- What do we know?
- What are we doing?
- Why are we doing it?
- When are we doing it?
- Where is it happening?
- How much will it cost?

Goals and actions are the building blocks for your marketing plan. They outline the main purpose of the marketing plan and help you align your individual efforts with business goals. The action steps should funnel up to meet the goals. You should construct them this way so that you justify all actions and know that all actions you take will help you meet your marketing plan's goals.

Goals

A goal is a specific statement about what you want to achieve with your marketing plan. Set goals to make sure you don't delude yourself into thinking that you're making progress when you're not. Goals keep you on track and help you hold yourself accountable to results. The best way to create goals that inspire action is to adopt the widely used SMART goal framework.

- **Specific** – Think of this as the subject of what you are trying to accomplish. Is it revenue, customers, web traffic? Focusing on one thing will increase the effectiveness of your marketing actions.
- **Measurable** – A goal is measurable if you can assess it with numbers, figures, or percents. In other words, "by how much" are you going to do something?
- **Attainable** – An attainable goal should be challenging, but realistic.
- **Relevant** – Align the goal so that it benefits something specific to your business.
- **Time-bound** – Frame the goal with a deadline to keep yourself accountable.

When your goals are SMART, they're more effective at inspiring meaningful action. Here is an example of what happens when you take a goal and make it SMART:

Not SMART: Grow my social media.

SMART: Grow my Twitter following by two thousand by the end of the year to increase awareness.

Much better, right? The second goal is much clearer than the first. We can attest that framing your goals to be SMART can make a huge difference in clarifying the objective and making it more likely to be achieved. Ready to make some SMART goals? Here are some examples of goals that you might find helpful:

1. Change:	2. What:	3. By how much:	4. By when:
Increase	Website traffic	5%	In one week
Decrease	Social media followers	10%	In one month
	Repeat customers	15%	In one year
	New customers	20%	
	Profit	25%	
	Sales	30%	

Think of your goals as something set in stone, but you can decide how big you want them. They can range from thirty days to five years as long as you can fit marketing actions in that can accomplish something notable. Simply planning a quick goal for the sake of saying you did something is letting yourself down. This is your opportunity to challenge yourself with something new and we want to see you find a goal that is realistic and something thing you want to strive for.

SMART Goals Get Us Out Of The Denial Trap

One of the biggest challenges small companies face when considering how to use social media is thinking that they're able to do it all. By doing it all, we mean running the business, making sales, fulfilling client orders, AND running Facebook, Twitter, LinkedIn, Instagram, Pinterest, YouTube, blog, and e-newsletter. We've learned that when people say that they're doing all those things effectively, something eventually suffers. Only the most insane are actually able to do all those things well at the same time. We doubt you are insane, or want to be insane. Obviously time management is critical, however, having good goals and making them realistic will keep your marketing workload realistic, and within reason.

Sticking to SMART goals can bring you out of this denial mode and into reality by forcing you to come to terms with what you're *actually* able to accomplish. If your goal is SMART, you'll contend with a time deadline and measurement. This means that by the time the time's up, you will either have succeeded, or you will have to actually admit to yourself as a leader that you missed your goal. Now, no one hits his or her goals all the time, but being able to admit to yourself when you don't hit your goals is the best way to hit them next time.

When starting with a SMART goal, realize you have a goal that works for you. If it fits your business and your abilities, then you have the best chance of obtaining it. As we said, failure happens, and yeah, it sucks to fail, but it isn't the end of the world. Many of us are so afraid of failure that it causes anxiety. What we found is those who are afraid of failure, are also afraid of learning new skills. This is how many businesses truly fail, because they get so beat down that they give up entirely. Failure gives us the best opportunity to learn and inspire us to bounce back twice as strong!

Actions

Actions, which some people call tactics, are individual tasks in a plan. They describe exactly what is going to be done to reach the goals of the marketing plan. Each action has a unique purpose, but are all aimed at achieving your SMART goals. Here are some example actions:

- Setting up a promotional schedule to promote on social media or your website.
- Using email marketing to market to promote new products or services
- Learning about Google Analytics so you can improve your website.
- Putting on a free webinar to generate leads.

When you build out your actions, make sure you get as detailed a possible about how you want to carry out each action. For instance, if you want to engage in e-mail marketing, you should talk about how to send out the emails: Will you buy an email marketing platform or send them out personally to specific customers from your business e-mail account? If you want them to look professional, but lack design skills or the time to make them, consider looking at an email marketing platform. Many exist to help you achieve your goals. How often you will send out emails, not to mention what content each email will contain, will need to be planned for.

Think of your actions as a script in a play. You want each line to flow in a specific order. The best plays are the ones that are well-rehearsed and organized. Planning out everything and even preparing things ahead of time will pay off in the long run. You definitely don't want to be scrambling halfway through your marketing plan if a giant, unforeseen obstacle comes up.

Campaigns

Marketing plans are great tools for outlining the direction of your business's marketing strategy for time periods of six to twelve months. But a lot can change in your business over that time. You might come up with new initiatives, new promotions, new products or services, or a host of other ideas. So, while your marketing plan will guide your overarching strategy and major goals, campaign plans can help you strategize and plan smaller initiatives of thirty to ninety days.

So, what makes a campaign plan different from a marketing plan? Not much, really. They still consist of the same basic building blocks as a marketing plan: a SMART goal and actions. They're just done on a smaller time scale and timeframes outside of your SMART goal. Campaigns are designed to carry out a specific promotion and can relate to a specific action, but they are meant to use a separate time frame of promotion within your marketing plan.

While each campaign relates to your SMART goal and time frame, each is a specific effort. Think of them like an advertising campaign. Businesses will have their marketing plan drafted up, and in that marketing plan they will include specific advertising campaigns as part of their strategy. That is all they are.

When is the Plan Ready?

It isn't an easy question to answer and not something we can answer for you. If it is too detailed, chances are it might be difficult to execute. We have seen marketing plans be as short as a couple of pages and as long as fifty. The ultimate indicator of whether your plan is ready or not is if you think you have enough to make a significant impact.

Here are ten things to consider if your plan is ready:

1. The goals are realistic, achievable, and satisfy the needs of your business.
2. It includes enough actions to keep the business busy with marketing efforts.
3. The plan does not make you have second thoughts. Instead, you think it will create value.
4. You feel comfortable with the budget; even if it is more than you thought, you still feel good about it.
5. Your research gave you new insight about your business, your competitors, or your target audience.
6. Your plan gives you confidence.
7. Actions and tools work dependently, rather than independently of each other.
8. You have metrics that tell you whether your plan is working.
9. The plan is challenging, but not impossible to carry out.
10. It is organized well enough that a third party can understand it.

Only you will know when your plan is truly ready to be released into the world. But when the time is right, it can be a beautiful thing. Saddle up, partner. Because it's time to launch.

6

Launch: Executing The Marketing Plan

This is the time for you to look over the plan one last time and make any changes. Before hitting "Launch!" let's go over a few tips to help you succeed with your marketing plan and go cover any commonly forgotten steps.

Create a Baseline for Measuring

Before you do hit the launch button, compile all of your sales, web traffic, and social media statistics down on a single document. This will be your baseline so you can compare the results at the end of your marketing plan. Annotate any previous marketing actions. This will help resolve any outliers in your sales data.

Sales data is usually the best indicator for marketing plan performance, but sometimes the success of a marketing plan is gauged by the performance of other goals related to specific tools such as your website or increasing return customers.

Marketing Plan Calendar

A marketing calendar will plan out when specific tasks are due such as the design for an e-mail is completed, sending a tweet or a Facebook update, and the timelines for starting or stopping specific promotions. Another use for them is creating checkpoints for where your marketing plan should be at a specific time. For instance, if your goal is to increase revenue by twenty percent over the year, you want to track each month of sales in comparison to the previous year's sales data.

As you proceed throughout the book, we will make recommendations for how to include the upcoming marketing tools in your editorial calendar.

Resource Readiness

Do you have all the resources you need for the marketing plan? Resources can include everything from money, time, hired help to build a website, writing content or, purchasing a tool. Look at each of your actions and figure out exactly what you need. Are you able to do all of this on your own? If not, figure out who will be helping you and what are they responsible for.

While you're figuring this out, keep in mind that it is possible to use up all of your resources—whatever they are— quickly. Because of this, itemizing all the things that haven't been built and when they are needed will give you a good estimate of the resources needed for each. Referring back to the previous section with building a marketing calendar, adding these tasks in there will keep everything on track.

When completing these tasks for your marketing actions, be mindful of when you might be going over your estimated resources. Think about if this will have a long-term effect on other tasks or delay any marketing actions. If you have some buffer, you might not have a problem, but if you cannot commit any more resources, you might have to make the call and either launch with what you have or move on. Sometimes it is a relief to go with what you have, but as we said before, a marketing plan is nothing until it is launched.

Your Resource Readiness list can look something like this:

Name of task
1. Who is responsible for it?
2. Estimation of time to complete.
3. Other needed resources.
4. Is it a prerequisite for another task?

Breaking Down Goals into Manageable Chunks

It helps to start with a single strategy at a time. When everything needs to launch at once, you may be asking for trouble. Space out each of your actions throughout the time period set in your marketing plan so that you are not overwhelmed by slamming eight lanes of traffic into a single lane.

If you have help from within your business, delegate some of this out or hire new staff to assist you. With this new marketing plan, you might be able to earn enough revenue to pay for that much-needed staff member. Trying to do everything by yourself is a recipe for disaster. Sometimes it is better to reduce the workload for the sake of getting something done. You have already done so much work to get to this point, and watching your plan collect dust on the launchpad can be quite disheartening. It is OKAY to cut some stuff from the plan if that's what you need to do in order to get going more quickly.

As one of our idols, Arianna Huffington, once said, "The easiest way to finish a project is by dropping it."

7

Measure:
Measuring Performance

If a tree falls in the forest, and no one is around to hear it, does it make a sound? We've all heard this philosophical question before. It gets down to the fundamental question of the relationship between perception and reality. There's another version of this question: If a customer finds you on the web and decides to make a purchase, but you don't track it, did it ever happen?

Think about it. Unless you implement a way to measure the results of your marketing efforts, you are flying blind. You will not be able to make decisions on where to spend you marketing resources if you do not know what is working and what isn't. This is why it is so important to get your analytics in place.

Here are the top five reasons for measuring your marketing performance:

1. **You will understand where revenue comes from and where it doesn't.** If you discover that more money is coming from a specific referral program rather than social media, master the

referral program. Social media may still have value for you, but perhaps it requires additional nurturing before you can leverage it.

2. **You will find patterns.** Whether they are purchase patterns or how people find you, what you see will help create long-term strategies. If you see a majority of your customers coming from search engines, find out why and make it easier for more customers to find you.

3. **You will be able to forecast.** You can use these patterns to set forecasts. For instance, if you can repeat a promotion at a time similar to when you ran the promotion before, you will have a good expectation about the number of sales it will create.

4. **You will build better plans.** Using the information from measuring your previous plan, you will have a foundation of what works and doesn't work.

You will prevent, find, and fix problems. Encountering problems is bound to happen, and in order to fix them, you need to first find them. Routinely checking your web traffic, sales, email lists, and other information will help you prevent major problems from escalating.

And here are the top five obstacles:

1. **"I am too busy."** Everyone is busy. Too often people get caught up with executing the plan and not enough in the measurement of it. Always, always, ALWAYS set aside time to track your marketing. If you honestly are too busy, delegate it or hire someone to help. Many consultants can help with this and it won't cost you an arm and a leg.

2. **"I cannot afford it."** Whoa. You can do a lot of measuring for free. This should hardly be an excuse because you can track small-scale metrics that you manage internally. In some situations, you'll need software to track things or you'll need to hire additional staff to delegate the work. But before it comes to that, at least focus on the basics.

3. **"I don't know how to track that."** New skills are sometimes hard to acquire. Thankfully, classes exist to teach these skills. The best

way to learn is by doing. If you are motivated at least to pick up a "Dummies" book, try it for yourself.

4. **"I don't see the value in it."** If you have to answer to someone or deliver proof that things are working, numbers are your friend. Before disregarding measurement completely, prove yourself wrong by trying a little experiment.

5. **"This is stupid."** It is easy to get frustrated, and yes, measuring performance can be overwhelming. Not matter what the stress is, everything will be okay, we promise. Instead of giving up altogether, scale back, downsize, or pivot your efforts. Giving up means all your efforts will be for nothing.

How to Make Measuring Your Performance Easy

Measuring performance is critical. To put in perspective, ask yourself, "Do I want to know if all that time and money I've devoted to my marketing helps?" Understanding how your marketing is doing does not require fancy software or a huge marketing team. Every company, regardless of size, can do *something* to identify how their marketing is doing. Take Lee Aase, director of Mayo Clinic Center for Social Media, as an example. Each week, his team creates a simple manual report. This means logging into each platform and grabbing statistics, such as how many likes, retweets, downloads, and views occurred. These weekly reports are part of the long-term understanding of how their social media is working.

Before Lee had even dreamed of the clinic's social media center, he began bringing the clinic's expertise to the public by providing a daily segment to radio stations covering various topics related to Mayo Clinic, such as new treatments and research. He interviewed doctors and provided an edited segment to the radio stations. In September 2005, he started publishing these short radio segments online, an effort that resulted in an average of nine hundred podcast downloads a month.

Given that the main publication venue was radio and the secondary publication venue was the web, the segments that Lee created for radio had to be short to make room for the other radio segments. And this limited the value the clinic could share. So Lee and his team thought about how to create more value from these podcasts without increasing effort. Then it dawned on them to just publish the interviews in their entirety. Since they already had the interviews with the Mayo doctors, they decided to make the whole conversations available on these podcasts to the public. By October of 2005, they were averaging seventy-four thousand downloads a month. That's an increase of over 8,200 percent! All they had to do was track downloads.

With the popularity growth of their podcasts, Lee and his team learned that once people have find interesting topics, they wanted longer, richer content. As interest grew, they proposed using new social media tools. In 2007, they started their first Facebook page and YouTube channel, and in 2008 they established a presence on Twitter. By 2009, they launched their first major blog. With the support of their leadership (mostly pushing them to grow), they founded the Mayo Clinic Center for Social Media. With their wide range of social media tools, they have been able to connect with patients, researchers, outside health organizations, and doctors across the globe. This catalyzed the growth and reach of the Mayo Clinic, helping the clinic bolster the reputation it enjoys today.

The idea is that when you make small, but long-term changes to your habits, the results compound over time. It is quite a simple thing if you think about it. But the problem that marketers or business owners run into is not seeing results right away. Starting a Twitter account might not get results in the first six months, but consistently keeping up with your Twitter account will allow you to build your results over time. No matter what marketing goal you're undertaking, it's important to remember that small tasks done consistently over time can produce great results. We see this all the time when businesses finally develop their social media so it reaches critical mass.

Measuring your marketing performance is partly related to your SMART goal. Then you can infer what information you want to measure. A common way to measure marketing performance is to build a sales funnel since most goals relate to increasing profit. The sales funnel assumes that each metric is somehow dependent on the others. For example, let's say the marketing team for a business gathers information on 1,200 decision makers in its target audience and sends each of them a media kit. The goal is to drive them to a webpage and get them to register for an online demo. The offer is a chance to win an Apple iPad if they sign up.

Of the 1,200 people that receive the mailer, thirty visit the webpage. Of those thirty, eight sign up for the demo and become eligible for the free iPad. Of those eight, five attended the demo, and from those five came three sales that totaled $150,000 in revenue. The total cost of the whole campaign was approximately $5,000.

Never use revenue as a way to calculate your ROI. This is because that $150,000 isn't all profit—it still costs the software company money to deliver that $150,000 in value to the customers. Let's assume that the company earns $20,000 in profit from the $150,000 in revenue.

So: $20,000 (Gross profit) - $5,000 (Campaign cost) / $5,000 (Campaign cost) = 3 dollars earned for every dollar spent (ROI of 300 percent).

That was an example for a specific campaign. What about a year-long marketing campaign? The same can be applied. Just replace campaign costs with total marketing costs for the year. Some companies also like to look at the ROI produced by each tool they use, and so compare the ROI from the web to advertisements, etc.

Everything in business and marketing is scalable. This is important for planning for two reasons. Firstly, in terms of discipline and personal development, scalability underlies the importance of the day-to-day activities involved in building your following. Learning how to take advantage of every little customer interaction to consistently treat customers like gold is often more effective than planning a fancy campaign. Your success in doing this is less dependent on where you start than on both how much you can endow seemingly small actions with impact and how long you can keep yourself going in the right direction.

Exponential growth explains the importance of creating a repeatable system. Instead of focusing on how to please the masses, narrow your focus to really please a single customer; this essentially amounts to planning for small, consistent interactions. Once you've got a system to please one customer, it's only then that you can plan to please all your potential customers.

Notice that if your small, consistent activities don't satisfy at the "single-customer" level, you'll only be relying on big things for growth, and this kind of improvement doesn't grow exponentially with time. Knowing your metrics by implementing a manageable reporting schedule is essential to making sure that all parts of your marketing operation are running efficiently and performing as expected.

8

Repeat-Finding the Actions That Work, and Using Them Again!

Considering the time period for your marketing plan, what do you want to do for your next marketing plan? What; you really thought you only needed to do only one? Of course not! Each year (or whatever time period you use) you should reevaluate and implement a new marketing plan. This is absolutely crucial for your business.

What we want you to avoid is something similar to the beach-season diet. That's when you work really hard to get into that nice swimming suit but then, when you get back from vacation, you slouch off and wait until next year to get back into shape. How productive is that? If you at least keep a foundation throughout the year, you'll find that it's much easier to slip back into that swimming suit and not even have to worry about it at all come next vacation. *Ooo la la!*

Debrief: Deciding What to Cut, Continue, Cultivate?

Before deciding what in your current plan you should change for next year, you should figure out if you need to create a new goal. After reviewing your marketing plan's goals and actions, put them into three categories: cut, continue, and cultivate. This will give you a foundation for your next marketing plan.

Cut

Did you find that some of your marketing actions just didn't work well at all? Before you cut it completely, evaluate whether the action just needs additional nurturing or adjustment. We find that some businesses expect their marketing to work all the time or right away, and if it doesn't, it is the fault of the marketing. Sorry to say that success doesn't happen overnight. It takes time to hit a critical mass.

So let's say you've done your due diligence and you find that an action just produced crap. Then you can cut it. But cutting right away may not be feasible. Instead, take a slow approach to removing pieces of your marketing plan is better.

Another reason to cut some of your marketing plan is if you find that one of your actions performs above your expectations, but the other actions don't perform at all. In this case, cut out the bad marketing actions and recycle those resources into the actions that are proven. Just like DipYourCar, start with one tool and master it. When you've mastered it, move on to the next one.

Continue

So you found something that works; keep it going! Think about if there is anything you can improve in your marketing actions. Some of you may think "Why fix something that isn't broken?" We don't necessarily mean change it significantly, but add on to it. For instance, if you have a marketing action to engage in social media tools, try expanding on it by spending more time tweeting, creating conversation with customers, updating your Facebook page with new offers and products, make more videos on YouTube, etc. This is also an opportunity to experiment. You already have something that is consistent and that gives you a great platform to try something new or add on to your marketing actions.

Cultivate

Things don't always go as planned. Some marketing actions require additional nurturing before yielding any positive impact. The idea is that the long-term goal will pay off once you nurture what is necessary to achieve the goal, and it is hard to predict which parts of your marketing plan will work and which won't. You may need to depend on intuition to decide whether you should cultivate and adjust any particular part of your marketing plan. And don't be afraid to change something or to continue nurturing something else. Finding the right rhythm to shout in the right direction takes time, but when you finally get it, you will be glad you kept pushing ahead.

Conclusion: Go, Go, Go!

Get excited because you now understand how to build a marketing plan! Remember, you don't need anything special or in grand length. A good marketing plan explains what is going to happen, but a great one will explain why. Even if you have just a couple of pages of what you are doing and why, that is okay! Don't feel pressured that you need to inspect every bit of your business to get a marketing plan done either. Some businesses need to do a little extra because they live in highly competitive environments. If your business competes with many other businesses, go the extra mile. You will be blown away by how far a little bit more research or a little bit more depth in you marketing plan can go.

As we said before, the worst kind of marketing plan is one that never launches. In other words, if you can't get yourself to scale a hill, don't climb a mountain. Pushing yourself to make your marketing a stronger aspect of your business is the other requirement. We want you to push yourself, but you need to draw that line where you don't want to go over. Yes, this is all hard work. However, the secret is making it enjoyable; if you feed off of happy customers or when you break your sales record, use it to inspire your marketing!

You probably have some great ideas to for your marketing plan. Before you start nailing everything together, you probably need a few tools, unless you have iron hands and saw-toothed fingers. The next section, Tools, will bring your marketing plan to life by identifying the best tools to meet your SMART goals and how to best use them.

Part II – Tools

In the previous section, we talked about the fundamentals of creating a plan that actually gets used. We've laid out the framework for defining your plan's goals and actions; this is a particularly handy way to think about how to organize your marketing strategy. Before you sit down and bang out your plan, it's a good idea to get the lay of the marketing landscape.

In the previous section, we helped you identify the what, when, where, and—most importantly—the why of your marketing. Now that you can justify why to use social network W and advertising channel X, to blog about Y, and tracking it with Z, it is time to get down to the how.

That's what this section is all about: the *how*.

Now that you're inspired to build a marketing plan, it's time to load up your arsenal. There are TONS of tools available for you to plug into your plan. Building a deadly marketing arsenal is all about two things: picking out the tools and *actually* being real with yourself about how much work it is to use the tools you've picked. Yes: we know how tempting it is to try to use every tool, system, social network, blogging platform, analytics dashboard, and Twitter-Facebook-Instagram-brand-o-matic under the sun to create a huge monster of a plan right off the bat (we, too, suffer from severe cases of shiny object syndrome). Not all of these tools are for everyone.

If you're running a business, we bet that you have a pretty hefty to-do list, with "social media" or "website" sitting right there at the bottom. For many companies, online marketing is one of those things that they always want to get to "later." The key to bringing "later" into "now" is to choose a plan that's both aggressive in its goals but feels very doable. Building yourself a mountain of a marketing plan will only do one thing: ensure that you can never get up the nerve to climb it today. As many a business coach has told us, "Done is better than perfect." Those words are just as true about marketing plans as about anything else in business.

Part of shouting in the right direction is picking the right tools for the job, and not biting off more work than you can chew. If you make yourself a marketing plan that you don't want to actually implement, then you're not really shouting that effectively, are you?

Regardless of your experience with digital marketing, you'll need to choose a set of tools to help get your message out. Anyone who has begun to do some searching for marketing tools has probably come to terms with the fact that there are roughly a gazillion[1] of them out there. Some have reported to us that social media marketing seems just so overwhelming because of the sheer number of different things they can be spending their time on. From getting likes on Facebook, to tweeting, to writing blogs, to sending e-mail newsletters, the amount of time commitment can seem overwhelming.

Our goal in helping you shout in the right direction is to help you to choose a plan that works for you. In our section on planning, you learned the importance of justifying your actions. If all you want to do is run a Facebook page and blog, have at it. We won't judge. For some small companies, that may be a great strategic move. Your marketing has to work for you, though. It has to fit your company, your message, and the way you think and work. Don't let that flashy business down the street that has it all together—you know the one—peer pressure you into doing something that isn't right for you. Making a conscious, forward-looking plan for your business and marketing is the best way to make sure you stay on course.

The point of the tools section is to familiarize you with the major types of tools available for you use. You don't have to use them all; hardly anyone does. By the end of this section, though, you'll be able to make a sound judgment about which tools you would like to incorporate into your plan, based on a broad understanding of the whole world of web marketing.

---

1   *Based on a recent study from Lehnen, Rosener, et al. Just kidding.*

9

Why Each Social Media Site Is Like Its Own Country

People often ask us which social media sites they should use for their marketing. Then we ask them, "If you could live in any country in the world, where would you want to live?" These two questions have surprising similarities. Like different countries, social media sites have different cultures that affect how people there do business and interact.

Think about it. Each network has a different population. Different groups of people use them, some have more people than others, and people use them more or less frequently. They have different languages and lingo. For example, many people who try Twitter for the first time go into culture shock trying to pick up on the "secret language" of RTs, #FFs, and more. As it turns out, every social network is like this. Just like traveling to a different nation, starting up a presence for your business on a new social network requires spending some time interacting with the locals to learn the customs.

Getting your audience to resonate with your target marketing is imperative for being effective on the web, but it is also important to be mindful of the social network's culture. What would make a huge splash on Twitter might not get a second look on LinkedIn. Each channel has its own personality, different types of media that it emphasizes, and different demographics of users with different motivations for using the channel.

As part of customizing your strategy for the culture of the medium you're using, consider the dynamics of how content is shared through and/or on the platform. For example, if you're considering a Facebook campaign, you'll want to get the most eyeballs on your content. Part of the planning should involve asking, "How do I get my customers to share this with their network, and how do I make it valuable to share or interact with?" Ask yourself, "Is it as part of an active effort (such as sending a message with my page to their followers)? Or as a passive result of interacting with my content (such as a Facebook "Like" appearing in a customer's timeline for his or her network to see passively).

A Word of Caution about These Descriptions

As part of our aim to give you a full overview of social media, we have complied the best practices of, along with our cultural observations for, each of the following social networks. That said, it seems like a new update to one of the big four websites comes out every week! As is the problem with the fast-paced world of the web, information quickly changes, and with it changes the approach we take to our marketing.

This is why we find it so exhausting to keep up with every news release about what's changing with all the social networks; it's truly never-ending. And if we're frustrated with it, we can bet you're frustrated as well. The solution to this problem is to focus on the core of what makes your marketing successful. While hanging on every announcement from Facebook about new layouts may help a bit, it's even more important to develop priorities about what actually gets you results. In other words, care not about the changes—care about the strategy. Ultimately, knowing how to actually use the platforms is important, but not as important as knowing *why* you're doing what you're doing.

The same thing goes for hopping on the bandwagon when a new social network pops up. It seems like every month a new hot social media site comes out, and we poor marketers are pressured to stay ahead of the curve by building a presence on it. Poppycock! Well, mostly. Admittedly, keeping current with trends is important. But at the same time, most business owners need another social network to keep up with like they need a hole in the head.

There is hope, however. Take these descriptions with a grain of salt, but also focus on the process of finding the common ground between them. No matter what changes on Facebook, or how many times LinkedIn re-arranges its layout, the basic principles of marketing with social media stay the same. If you learn to clarify your business goals as they relate to social media, you will be able to adapt your strategy quickly when things inevitably change.

As you navigate the descriptions below, keep this in mind: A hot new social network will always hit the scene, and the ones that are currently out there will continue to change. While the information that follows covers the basics of what the most popular social networks are all about, we don't cover each in (excruciating) detail. But that should be enough for you to gain important and fundamental familiarity with each of the biggest sites. You never know; you may want to set up shop there some day. No matter how much you think, "This isn't for me," or "This won't work," it's doable. We promise. We know you can do it, because you're awesome.

Use This Section to Make an Editorial Calendar

If you've done any research on social media and digital marketing, you've likely come across the term "editorial calendar." It's a simple tool for helping you keep track of all the content coming out of your business, on what network, and who's responsible for making it happen. In other words, it is a calendar identifying the content (e.g., videos, images, blog posts, updates, links to other sites, calls to action) you plan to post each day. As you go through the profiles of the different social media chan-nels, take note of the ones you want to take on for your marketing. Each will have a *reasonable communication goal for your editorial calendar,* one that will help you determine how much time you might spend on that network if you choose to take it on.

How [Insert Social Network] Helps Your Business

Though every social network has a radically different culture, basic ideas and principles determine how any social network under the sun can help your business. It essentially boils down to two things:

1. Getting eyeballs on you (likes, followers, connections, group members, subscribers, etc.).
2. Giving the eyeballs something creative that they like (images, videos, events, webinars, case studies, blogs, posts, tweets, and the like).

That's it. Seems pretty easy when you get down to it, right? This is where your creativity comes in. The task before you is simple, but you choose how creatively to execute it. Each social network has different tricks to help you, based on its culture and the way people use the network. Here are a few observations to help you get the most out of "your eyeballs," and get you shouting in the right direction.

10

Facebook

www.facebook.com

Ahh, Facebook. It's everyone's go-to topic when talking about social media. Because it is the largest social network, no discussion of digital marketing would be complete without it. It's got more than 1.19 billion active users.[1] It's huge.

The unfortunate consequence of its hugeness is that every digital marketer worth his or her salt is competing with you to win Facebookers' attention. And that attention span is small. First and foremost, people are on Facebook to connect with their friends and families, not businesses and brands. The average user likes only nine companies.[2] So what does it take to be one of those nine? How can you be interesting enough so that people will want to hear from you, when they are primarily on Facebook to hear from people they know? That, my friend, is our biggest challenge in social media: putting out compelling content.

So, how do you shout louder (and in a way and direction that entices those eyeballs) than all your competitors so people who aren't primarily

---

1   *http://investor.fb.com/releasedetail.cfm?ReleaseID=802760*
2   *Study by Exact Target, Fall 2011.*

interested in giving you the time of day do just that? You've just got to be better than everyone else, of course. Here are a few thoughts that might help:

How You Build Your Following

Encourage people in your network to visit your Facebook page and click the "Like" button. Once Facebook users click "Like" on your page, they will receive your status updates alongside the postings of their personal friends and the other pages they like.

How to Get More People to See Your Posts

All right. There's a darker side to Facebook that you should probably know about. Over the past year, we've been getting reports that businesses using Facebook have been experiencing declining results. Why might this be? Not every person who likes your Facebook business page sees every post you put out. While this may seem like common sense, it's beginning to become quite a problem.

When you publish an update on your business Facebook page, the people who have liked your page see your post in their news feed when they log in. That's the general idea—when it works.

In reality, Facebook filters the posts displayed to its users based on what it determines they want to see. The algorithm that does this filtering is called the EdgeRank algorithm: Understanding it better will help you better understand how to grow your page.

Get More Eyeballs on Your Posts by Understanding Facebook's EdgeRank Algorithm

Imagine for a moment that you work for Facebook. When you're putting Facebook together, your goal is to display the most important Facebook updates to users when they log on. You're then tasked with designing a system that can determine how much a user wants to see a particular piece of content. The EdgeRank algorithm decides what to show in a user's feed based on three factors:

- <u>Affinity:</u> The more a user likes, shares, and comments on your updates, the more affinity he or she has to you. Specifically, if a user likes your stuff, he or she will see more of it.
- <u>Content Type:</u> Some types of content work better than others on Facebook. Images and videos, for example, fare better in EdgeRank than text or third-party app updates.
- <u>Recency:</u> People want to see updates that are recent. The newer a post is, the more likely it is to be viewed.

Knowing this, if you want to get more eyeballs on your Facebook posts, keep in mind what Facebook uses to determine who sees them.

The "Preaching to the Choir" Effect

One tangible effect of EdgeRank on Facebook marketing has been to change the focus of what types of customers can be targeted effectively. Let us explain.

The "affinity" aspect of EdgeRank means that people who like, comment, and share your content are more likely to see your content in the future. Yet in practice, the people who like, share, and comment the most are *already* close networking colleagues. Though this might seem like a good thing, it means that you are more effective at marketing to people who already know you well—and interact with you—than you are with people who you don't know you well.

This is the core of the "preaching to the choir" effect. Because your message is more likely to reach people who have a history of liking you, it's less likely to reach people whom you have just met (despite the fact that they are the ones we marketers want to reach the most)!

While this is a potential problem, it can be turned into a positive if used correctly. Insights like this underline the importance of driving people to like your content so they will see your future content more often. In order to shout in the right direction, we must recognize that when we put out our messages on Facebook, we're not necessarily targeting everyone who likes the page: we're targeting people who already have a history of liking us. Writing your posts for them will go a long way to beefing up your results.

Shout in the Right Direction on Facebook by Gaining Clarity about Your Target Audience

One of the most common problems businesses have on social media is trying to reach everyone. The truth is, if you're a small company, the only advantage you have over larger companies (with larger budgets) is that you don't have to reach everyone. Because you're smaller, you can focus only on the prospects and customers that are a perfect match.

This gives you a huge advantage on the web, because you don't have to waste time with people who aren't reasonably going to buy from you.

When you're planning your Facebook page—what to call it, how to design the page, what you're going to post on it, how you're going to promote it—think about that perfect marketing fit. Ask yourself:

- Do I have a clear vision of my "perfect-fit" audience?
- Does that audience really use Facebook to interact with companies? How do I know?
- What kinds of content does my perfect-fit audience care about?

By having out-of-this-world focus on what your perfect fit wants to hear from you on Facebook, you'll be well on your way to a growing and thriving Facebook page.

A Reasonable Communication Goal for Your Editorial Calendar

- Post content once per day, with a focus on pictures and videos.
- Switch up your profile, cover photo, and other information once per quarter.

11

Twitter

www.twitter.com

Even though Twitter is one of the better-established social networks, many marketers find themselves at a loss when trying to develop a strategy for reaching and engaging Twitter users.

When the topic of Twitter comes up in conversation, we get lots of:

- I don't "Twitter."
- Are my customers even on Twitter?
- Does anyone really understand Twitter?

Yes, Twitter is one of those networks that requires you to climb a bit of a learning curve. And, yes, not every business needs a Twitter strategy (especially if customers aren't on it). But don't count Twitter out too quickly: There's some business value to be had on this platform if you use it correctly.

The Culture of Twitter

We're often asked, "Can I just post everything I post to Facebook onto Twitter?" Most often, the right answer is no, especially if the information is something you want to make sure your audiences knows about. On Twitter, everything is immediate. Because tweets come by in a streaming timeline, you can't assume that your followers "hear" everything you say. The half-life of a link shared on Twitter is about two hours; this means that for every two hours after you release your tweet, the number of people who see it reduces by half. Because everything goes by so quickly, users tend to treat Twitter more like a river (to use a water analogy). When you want to take a swim in the river, it's there for you to enjoy and interact with. But when you're away from the water grilling on the beach, the river is still there rushing by (and it's okay to let it go).

You're Probably Not Tweeting Too Much. Really

People who tweet between ten and fifty times a day have more followers than those who tweet more or less, with the peak at twenty times per day.[1] The average Twitter user even tweets a little more than four times per day. So don't worry about tweeting too much. Unless you're tweeting more than fifty times a day, it likely isn't a problem. Especially since new tweets get pushed down so quickly by ever newer ones, tweeting more each day is almost always likely to help more than it hurts. So, let 'er rip! Your community wants to hear you.

Branding Your Twitter Page: Personal, Company, or Both?

"Who am I talking to?" This seems like a simple question, but from a marketing and branding point of view, it has important impact. On Twitter (and all other social media platforms, for that matter), the customers you're connecting with want to be told how they should interact with you. One of the most fundamental ways to do this is to decide how to brand your account. Does the account represent your company as a whole? Does it represent you personally? Does it represent the profes-

1   http://blog.hubspot.com/blog/tabid/6307/bid/4594/Is-22-Tweets-Per-Day-the-Opti-mum.aspx

sional side of your personal identity (think of people who have strong personal brands)?

This may seem like a picky distinction, but it has a large impact on the things you might say, how you speak, the voice you use, and the ways that people want to interact with you. For example, a company Twitter profile would be right on target posting company news, announcements, and other promotions on behalf of the brand, but may get bogged down when having to engage in too many one-on-one conversations. Or consider this: people might reasonably expect a company profile to be managed by several people (and delegated to members of your team) but people can become offended if they find out that messages intended for your personal profile went to someone else and never reached you. On the other side of the coin, having a personal profile on Twitter that directly shows your brand's name instead of your company's is a great way to encourage a more personal connection with people in your network.

If your company has a number of employees, putting multiple profiles on Twitter also can serve as a way for you to allow all your employees to be on social media without giving everyone access to the official company profile. For example, at Tech Nick, Nick has a main Twitter account for the company—it's called Tech Nick Tips (@technicktips)—while he (@nickrosener) and each of his employees has his or her own in order to make more personal connections with clients, prospects, and the business's network.

Keep this in mind when you're setting up Twitter profiles for your company. Whether you choose to have a company profile, a personal profile, or both has a big effect on how people interact with you on the web.

How to Automate Some Things on Twitter without Pissing People Off

Understandably, busy professionals are often tempted to find different ways to save time on social media efforts. On Twitter, for example, one of the established ways to save some time is to automate some of the messages that go out. Several tools exist that help with automating your

Twitter profile to some extent by helping you schedule tweets (and accomplish other tasks as well) in advance.

This is all fine and good: we're all for efficiency and saving time. But automating your marketing comes with a warning. If you're not careful, you might end up alienating your audience, making your customers feel like you're not invested in the digital relationship, or worse, missing connections from potential customers who reach out to a system that you've automated and forgotten about.

If you want to explore the world of scheduling your tweets in advance, you have our blessing; just be smart about it. To be frank, there are a wide variety of opinions out there in marketing land about the best "automating your marketing" practices, but our take is that automating can be an effective strategy for improving the efficiency of your team—as long as you make sure you're never sacrificing the human interaction element (which is what social media is all about, anyway).

Think about a small consulting company that writes a weekly blog, and wants to use Twitter to promote its blog articles. The people responsible for getting company messages out there decide on a strategy: they'll tweet a daily quote from the weekly blog in order to bring people to the blog to read the whole article. They then consider whether they should go on to Twitter each day to send out the daily tweet manually, or use an automation system to schedule all the tweets at once. After carrying out this strategy manually for a few weeks, they also find that some of their customers like to respond to their shared quotes, and retweet the quotes to share with their followers. The social media manager at this company wonders whether automating this process and scheduling their tweets in advance is appropriate, given the audience's behavior.

Do the company's customers receive any added value by the social media manager physically logging on to Twitter each day to tweet out the quote? Not really. They would enjoy the tweet just as much had the manager automated the process. But the crux of the issue lies in responding effectively to the tweets and retweets that come out because of the daily quote. Automating this process would be a move forward only if the manager made sure that the company is still able to respond promptly to people who are responding and retweeting: often people do this by installing a smartphone application that alerts them when these things happen.

By making a commitment to keep a high standard for personal attention and interaction with its clients, this company was able to spend less time managing the daily blog quote promotions without sacrificing any of the marketing benefit. Keep this in mind if you go down the route of scheduling and automating tweets or other marketing communications.

Shout in the Right Direction on Twitter by Overcoming "Twitter Politeness"

I know what you're probably thinking, and we're not telling you to start being rude to your Twitter following. But we're not exaggerating when we say that professional politeness gets in the way of successful marketing on Twitter.

Think of what happens when you follow someone new for the first time. That person follows you back, thanks you for following him or her, and politely says how glad he or she is to meet you online. This person may even throw in an exclamation point or two.

This might seem all fine and good, but you can be sure that your new followers won't remember who you are two minutes from now. You've both made polite Twitter conversation, but no one made a significant connection.

So many people are on Twitter that it's impossible to have a deep meaningful relationship with all of them, but superficial followers aren't going to spread your content and tell everyone how great of a Twitter networker you are.

It's your job as a marketer to get past mere Twitter politeness, make real connections, and build raving fans. The key to getting past Twitter politeness is to focus on creating that real connection as quickly as possible.

Even though the average Twitter user may follow a few hundred people, most only actually interact regularly with a small subset of those whom they follow. For these lucky few people, users will memorize their Twitter handle, notice when their content comes across their feed, and go out of their way to share the content, making a point of reaching out to those special accounts that they care about.

When you're out there building your Twitter following, keep this in mind. Building followers is great, but building real Twitter relationships is even better. Followers with whom you have this kind of relationship are the ones who will really help you build your brand and convert to sales.

A Reasonable Communication Goal for Your Editorial Calendar

- Tweet once daily on each account that you're officially promoting.

12

LinkedIn

www.linkedin.com

Linkedin is one of our favorite social networks: It is, and continues to be, a very profitable source of business leads for us. But we know that people have lots of misconceptions about LinkedIn, especially when it comes to marketing. Many business owners we talk to view LinkedIn as a platform for helping people get jobs, but nothing more. If you find yourself falling into this line of thinking, take a moment to open yourself up to think about LinkedIn in a new light: LinkedIn is for so much more than finding a job.

LinkedIn is a professional networking site letting you build a network and communicate and engage with people in that network. Like all social media platforms we've talked about, it is easy to waste countless hours in undirected social media activity without having a strategy. Here are some pointers to consider that will help you keep on track and make your social efforts on LinkedIn more profitable.

Much like Facebook, LinkedIn has both individual profiles and company pages. Just to be clear, we're talking mostly about individual profiles in this section. While it's true that some companies have a company page on LinkedIn, we have usually found that people are more interested in interacting with *people* rather than *pages* on LinkedIn.

Start with an Optimized Profile

One of the first things you'll want to do with your LinkedIn account is spend some time completing your profile. If you've been in social media for long, you've likely come across the topic of search engine optimization (SEO), which is the process of optimizing your website to attract traffic from search engines. Most people think of SEO solely in terms of search engines like Google or Bing, but LinkedIn also has a search engine that LinkedIn users often search in order to find providers, give referrals, and network. To make sure that LinkedIn users searching for services you provide can find your profile, make sure to do the following to optimize your profile:

To make sure that LinkedIn users searching for services you provide can find your profile, make sure to do the following to optimize your profile:

1. Choose a descriptive headline that includes pertinent keywords. For example, "Owner at Tech Nick Creative" would not be as effective as "Digital Marketing Strategic Planner, WordPress Developer, or Certified Social Media Strategist at Tech Nick Creative."
2. Fill out your education, job experience, and other areas to 100-percent completion. Completed profiles show up more often in search results.
3. Get a professional headshot taken for your profile. Though this doesn't have a huge effect on search engine optimization, having a compelling headshot will work wonders in getting more people to pick you out of a huge list of people they might connect with.
4. When filling out your summary, try to strike a balance between being conversational and personal, adding relevant keywords to your profile, and having a clear call to action about the types of people you with whom you seek to network.
5. Start up a campaign to get recommendations from people you

have worked with: Getting more recommendations (which are different from endorsements) will help you convey your expertise and your history of satisfied clients.

6. Trick out your profile with all the fancy doodads and whizbangs that LinkedIn provides. Adding things like "Volunteer Experience and Causes," "Organizations," "Courses," and "Publications" serves to make your profile more complete and interesting.

If you follow these guidelines, along with some common sense, you'll be well on your way to a seriously robust LinkedIn profile designed to get results.

Join Interesting Groups and Demonstrate Your Leadership

Now that you've gotten your profile complete and up to date, you will find that potential partners and prospects are able to find you much more easily online. But, as mentioned before, LinkedIn is more than just a glorified résumé in the cloud: it's all about networking and leveraging your network. Using LinkedIn's groups feature is a great way to create new connections, expand your network, and gain some notoriety and leadership in the online world.

LinkedIn groups are LinkedIn's way of helping people gather around a common interest. There are groups that surround industries (LinkedIn Accounting, LinkedIn Entertainment, and Social Media Marketing), job functions (LinkedHR, The Project Manager Network, Retail Industry Professionals Group), local areas (LinkedMinnesota, Link Up Wisconsin, Florida Careers Networking and Jobs), and all manner of niche groups and combinations. If you have a certain target market in mind, it's almost guaranteed there exists a group in which you can find them. If not, you can create your own.

When it comes to LinkedIn groups, there are two broad strategies to use to build your network:

1. Connecting with your peers to build an industry network and keep up on your skills and knowledge.

2. Connecting with your potential prospects and customers by joining groups that don't describe *you*, but describe *them*.

You may want to consider using both of these strategies, but whatever you are pursuing at the moment will help you decide which groups to approach, and how to interact with the group while you're there.

Getting involved with groups is a great way to build name recognition and notoriety for your brand, especially if you're just introducing yourself to the online scene.

As a previous manager for a large LinkedIn group (28,000+ members), Nick also can tell you that managers are often open to bringing promising group members on board to assist with managing the group. Keeping tabs of a large group is time-consuming. From approving and screening new members to moderating and spurring conversations on discussion boards, there's lots of work to go around. Luckily, if the group is large enough, there's lots of marketing potential to go around as well. You may have success showing an interest in group leadership to the managers of a group you've targeted. The worst they can do is say no, and the opportunities that come along with management privileges are nice. It was not uncommon for us as managers to reward volunteers by plugging their businesses in weekly announcements, partnering with them on their events, and opening up prime speaking slots.

Get Creative with Finding New LinkedIn Contacts in Real Life

Some of the best opportunities to connect online come from chance interactions in the real world. LinkedIn is a great way to follow up with those interactions without seeming to overstep your bounds with a new contact. Giving a talk? Take those business cards you get afterward and connect on LinkedIn. Meet someone new and strike up a conversation at a coffee shop? Find that person on LinkedIn to stay in touch and grow that relationship. You never know who will turn into a good referral.

These are just a few examples of creative ways to use the in-real-life (IRL) interactions to spur a conversation and a LinkedIn connection. With some brainstorming, I'm sure you can come up with several more.

Consider Your Target Market When Making Connections

Executing a strategy on LinkedIn, like on most social networks, is all about evaluating the relationships available to you and cultivating the ones that pay off. If you're beginning to craft a LinkedIn network from scratch, take care when you begin to add people to your network: you'll get more people similar to them. It seems like a simple idea, but it's a profound effect of how LinkedIn works.

Many businesses have several different types of clients with whom they work, some of which are better than others. Furthermore, those same businesses often have many auxiliary people in their network, some of whom have lots of potential and others who don't.

When building your network, be conscious of the types of people you allow into your network from the start. If you begin to fill your network with too many of the wrong fit, it will be harder in the long run for your right fit to find you. Why? LinkedIn has complex algorithms that help suggest what connections people should make next, and one of the things it bases this suggestion on is the number of connections you have in common. By networking with too many of the wrong fit, you make it easier for those people to find you online in the future and you may be inadvertently stopping yourself from being able to reach those who are the right fit.

So, even if many of the people you're connecting with would be *okay, but not great clients* you may want to try to limit the number of those people in your network relative to the number of great-fit people. The more you focus your LinkedIn efforts on exactly the right fit of customer, the more you will get of them in the short term, and the easier it will be to find more of them in the long term.

Shout in the Right Direction on LinkedIn by Mastering all theWays to Communicate

To use LinkedIn to amplify your voice, use the following communication channels in LinkedIn:

1. Making status updates.
2. Sending direct messages to direct connections.
3. Sending InMail (paid e-mail) to people who aren't in your network.
4. Posting discussions in targeted groups with links to event information.
5. Creating relationships with managers of targeted groups to request that they send out an announcement to group members through LinkedIn (group managers are currently permitted to send out one announcement per week to the entire group).

A Reasonable Communication Goal for Your Editorial Calendar

- Make new connections from "people you may know" and your own marketing twice a month.
- Publish daily status updates.
- Interact with groups and discussions once per week.
- Update your profile once per quarter.

13

YouTube

www.youtube.com

YouTube is another of our favorite social networks because it becomes more relevant every day. YouTube is currently the second-largest search engine on the web, behind Google. More and more people use YouTube to find answers to the questions they would previously answer by reading a text document or blog article. And then there's the fact that online video is a great way to make a personal connection with your audience before they meet you. It is why DipYourCar was so successful. Fonzie used the platform to resonate with his audience by creating simple tutorial videos demonstrating how to use the product and convincing them that anyone can "dip" his or her car. He really engaged his audience by portraying himself as an average guy doing what he is passionate about. Even in today's digital age, there still is no substitute for someone being able to see your eyes when you speak.

Most of the discussion around how to use YouTube surrounds coming up with creative video concepts, finding a way to get videos produced, and getting viewers and traffic to the videos. Those who embark on a video strategy finds their own way of operating that they swear by; but here are some common threads we've found to help make your effort successful.

Have at Least One Really Great Professionally Produced Video

When it comes to video, one of the most common questions revolves around cost. You have likely seen your share of professionally produced videos, as well as some terrible home brewed ones. Choosing the right mix of professional and self-produced video is a core part of building a successful video strategy for your business. Professionally produced videos can sometimes cost from a few hundred to a few thousand dollars, but having at least one professional video can really elevate the status of your website or marketing in general.

That being said, most businesses would have only a few videos if they relied on professional videos alone: this is where self-produced videos can fit in. Once you have a professionally produced video to represent, say, the front page of your website, you may consider producing regular videos to distribute on your blog, your e-mail newsletters, and social media. Having a mixture of professional and DIY videos can bring you the best of both worlds: quality and quantity. Experiment to find the strategy that works best for you.

Make Your Blogs More Talkative with Video Blogs (Vlogs)

Despite the fact that the Internet and technology has enabled us to share information and connect with other humans more than ever before, there is something about face-to-face interaction that text alone just can't be replaced. Adding video to your blog brings back some of the "face-to-face" element to your marketing, and helps build stronger relationships with your audience (because they can actually look you in the eye).

Treat YouTube like you would a blog article; your videos should be both informative and entertaining. While there is some benefit to posting "sales only" videos, try to mix things up by including videos that add value to your subscribers and viewers. If you make videos that are as valuable as your blog articles are, you shouldn't have any trouble getting viewers and subscribers.

Produce Simple Videos to Promote Campaigns

Do you have something important to promote? One of the best ways to get your message across for a particular campaign or initiative is to create a video to help promote it. Such videos can be as simple as you looking at a webcam, telling viewers how excited you are to offer them the promotion you're mentioning. Not only will it be easier for your audience to comprehend than reading text, but viewers also will be able to sense your excitement, which will encourage them further to buy.

Shout in the Right Direction on YouTube by Making "Question Videos"

The most effective marketing videos take into account all the different avenues through which the video will bring in traffic. To get the most bang for your buck, consider the effect that the videos will have on SEO. Every day, people type questions into Google and other search engines related to your offerings: Why not publish videos that answer those questions?

Think of the questions that your clients ask most frequently. If your clients are asking those questions, you can be sure that your potential clients who have not yet met you are typing those questions into search boxes. By crafting your videos carefully and then describing them so they answer those questions, you increase the likelihood that you will end up ranking on search engines results pages when users ask those questions.

A Reasonable Communication Goal for Your Editorial Calendar

- Have one professionally produced video for your website
- Create one self-produced video per month for social media or your video blog.

14

Google+

plus.google.com

Despite the fact that Google+ is one of the newer social networks on the scene, it has quickly become a very important force in the social media space. You should pay attention to it for your marketing. With Google's huge user base and influence over how the world searches on the Internet, it has a large influence in shaping how the web uses social media, and how businesses connect with customers.

Specifically, Google is attempting to position its social network to incorporate the social web into the way people search and use mobile devices. This is especially relevant when you consider the three largest marketing trends on the web today coming together around Google+: social, local, and mobile.

Imagine yourself sitting at your office around one in the afternoon, stomach rumbling and past due for lunch. The prospect of a plate of spicy pad thai has been dancing around your mind for the past week, so you decide to pick one up. Never having had Thai food near your office before, you pull out your phone, fire up your web browser to Google.com, and search for nearby Thai restaurants. Without you having to do anything, your phone taps into your GPS location, your past browsing history, and other information about your preferences to make a recommendation for Thai restaurants nearby. Along with each listing is the Google+ local page of each restaurant, its customer reviews, and its most recent social media posts. As you can see, the combination of social, local, and mobile (or SoLoMo, if you're really trendy) is changing how people use the Internet to make purchasing decisions.

If nothing else, Google+ is well positioned to help your business have a presence at the intersection of these three new marketing trends, which may be a reason to have your company set up shop there.

Complete Your Profile, Cover Photo, and Links to Your Other Profiles

Just as with other social media platforms (notably, LinkedIn), Google+ has lots of areas for customization and linking to your other web properties. Take some time to make sure that your page is complete and visually appealing so when people find it on the web, it puts forward a good brand.

Try Out Google+ Hangouts

One of Google+'s defining features is called "Hangouts." Hangouts is an online multiway video chat feature that allows you to either have a conversation with several of your audience members online, or have a webinar- or radio-style live broadcast directly on Google+. Better yet, it's free.

If you have a topic that would gather people to listen to you speak, consider trying it on Google+ Hangouts. It's a rich, free feature that you have available to you on G+ that most other networks don't have.

+1's on Google+ Contribute to Your Search Engine Authority

For those of you who haven't spent much time on Google+, one of the ways users can interact with your posts on the platform is to click a button labeled "+1," which is a way to represent the popularity of a post. It's similar to clicking the "Like" button on a Facebook post.

On Google+, though, +1's have an additional effect: they actually help boost the authority of the referenced material in search engines. That's right folks; the more +1's a post gets, the higher that material will rank on search engine results pages. Google even goes as far as to customize your search results based on the things you and those in your G+ network have +1'ed in the past. Add this to the list of your potential strategic goals to get +1's on your posts, your search traffic will thank you for it.

Shout in the Right Direction on Google+ by Connecting to Google+ Local

If you have a bricks-and-mortar location (or one that you could display on the Internet as your home base), confirming your Google+ page with your physical location will go a long way to helping optimize your site for local search. All it takes is a few clicks, and sometimes a phone call or a letter from Google, but it's worth it.

A Reasonable Communication Goal for Your Editorial Calendar

- Post daily on your personal and company pages to engage your audience and differentiate yourself from others who do not post regularly.

15

Pinterest

www.pinterest.com

If there were a sign on the highway to the town of Pinterest, it would say "Welcome to Pinterest: Land of the Pretty." Pinterest is the place where people go to spend hours looking at photos, recipes, designs, and other things visual. If you have a brand that deals in anything visual, you may want to bring Pinterest into you social media strategy plan.

For those who haven't yet been exposed to the glorious world of Pinterest, it is a social network that claims to be "a tool for collecting and organizing things you love." Users do this by posting images of, and links to articles referring to, things that they love, and other users "pin" them to collections on their accounts, or boards. Businesses and brands can promote themselves on Pinterest by creating content for other users to collect and use for their boards.

Even though Pinterest may have fewer users than Facebook or Twitter, active Pinterest users spend TONS of time on it, with many reporting spending entire afternoons pinning, reading, and organizing their boards. If you want your business shine on Pinterest, here are some tips for helping make your account as pretty as possible.

Organize Your Boards for a Clean Look and Ease of Understanding

If you've been using Pinterest for a long time, you've likely accumulated lots of different boards and pins: many of them likely don't make sense together. Take some time to organize, edit, and tidy up your boards to make them more comprehensible and easier to understand for users who come to visit your page.

Help People Dream, Plan, and Get Inspired

When you're setting up shop on any social network, it's important to interpret the culture of the network, and do some research on how users prefer to use it. This will help you understand how people in the community get value out of using the platform and how you can best get their attention. One of the biggest reasons people use Pinterest is to dream about the future: their dream home, wedding, yard, food, vacation, and other things of that nature. You can plug into that by putting out content that others would want to collect on their boards as part of realizing their dream future.

Use Pricing Links When Appropriate

Take advantage of all the features that Pinterest offers to make your pins more interesting, and to help encourage users to purchase your products (if the pin you're referring to features a product for sale). One of these features it to include a price link in your pin, which will reinforce to users that the product is available.

Watermark or Brand Your Photos

What happens if the unthinkable occurs: people on Pinterest love your photo or image, and it goes wildly viral? How will people know that it came from your business? Some people even download photos and re-post them without attributing the original source, making it even harder to get your marketing benefit even if something does go viral.

You can remedy this by making sure to include your brand mark, your website URL, or your logo on your photos that you post on Pinterest. This will help make sure that your company stays front and center as your photos make their way across the Internet.

Shout in the Right Direction on Pinterest by Making Yourself a Really, Really Specific Niche

With the advent of blogging and social media, the Internet has made it extremely easy for anyone to become a content producer. Now that more and more people are getting online, people are becoming accustomed to the fact that they can find exactly what they're looking for, no matter how specific the niche is. This trend is called hypersegmentation. How else could you explain entire blogs and Pinterest pages dedicated to duct tape fashion?[1]

Luckily, this is one of the trends that can help small businesses more than large companies. In the hypersegmented Internet world, you can produce content for a small group of people and be able to find interested people across the globe. Pinterest is no exception. You may find more success on Pinterest by taking a hypersegmented approach. Have confidence in yourself to pursue a really, really specific topic: Contrary to common sense, you may have more success getting traction than if you try to tackle something really broad.

A Reasonable Communication Goal for Your Editorial Calendar

- Post something creative to one of your boards three to five times per week.
- Comment and interact with other Pinterest users three to five times per week.

---

1   *http://www.ducttapefashion.com/*
    http://pinterest.com/theduckbrand/duck-tape-fashion/

16

Instagram

www.instagram.com
Note: Instagram works better through its mobile application.

In the immortal words of Max from CBS's Sitcom 2 Broke Girls, "Twitter is stupid, and Instagram is Twitter for people who can't read." Okay, that's not necessarily true: Instagram is often a good addition to a legitimate marketing strategy. Out of all the social networks, we've found that Instagram is one of the ones that business owners have the toughest time incorporating into a marketing strategy. Even if it's tough, there is a way to make it work if you can be creative enough. Here are some best practices to get you going:

Help People Find Your Photos on Instagram by Loading Up on #Hashtags

Hashtags on Instagram work in a way similar to Twitter hashtags: Adding hashtags to your images helps categorize those images on Instagram and makes it easier for people who are exploring photos to find them. Don't be afraid to load your photo up with them.

Fewer People Are on Instagram, But That Could Be Good

Because Instagram is newer than the big four social networks, there definitely aren't as many people on it compared to Facebook. But that may be a good thing. The people who are on Instagram really have their stuff together, or they usually wouldn't be bothered to spend their time there.

In our experience, we've found that though there are less people on Instagram, there is also less competition for attention, and the people who do invest in Instagram (at least from a business standpoint) are people that others actually want to connect with.

Shout in the Right Direction on Instagram by Bringing People Together

The culture of Instagram centers around photography: many of its users are looking for a way to share their amateur photos, and want to find photographic inspiration from others.

One example of a company working the photography angle to get traction on Instagram is tena.cious Social+Design's Photo a Day Challenge[1]. Every month, tena.cious puts out a list of photo themes, one for each day of the month. Theme titles range from things like Gone, 4, Empty, and Hair to #Ladyfriends, Cold Drank, and Lazy Sunday. Their followers on Instagram take theme-related photos every day and post them to Instagram with the hashtag #TenaciousPicks. And people on Instagram love it!

Without knowing what to expect, tena.cious had six thousand hits to its website in the first month and ten thousand the second month, with more than 5,400 photos uploaded to Instagram with the #Tenacious-Picks hashtag.

Don't be afraid to be creative on Instagram, and see if you can figure out a way to build a community around your Instagram photos.

---

1   http://tenaciousedge.com/tenaciouspics/

A Reasonable Communication Goal
for Your Editorial Calendar

- Take advantage of as many photo ops as you can think of, roughly once a week.
- Put together an activity for your community to participate in.

17

How to Understand Social Media Culture

When you're building your social media profiles, you will quickly find that certain campaigns will land better on certain social platforms than on others. Trying to choose in advance which platform will help you drive your message can be difficult at times, especially if you're planning to do something particularly innovative or creative.

That being said, when you're planning your campaign, you'll need to use your judgment to make strategic decisions. In some ways, it's up to you to act like a social media anthropologist; researching and delving into a culture to be able to figure out how the culture works so you can fit in when you "travel to the country" to do marketing.

You may be faced with strategic decisions like:
- What platform(s) should I launch this idea on?
- Should I launch a campaign that features video or photos?
- Will people actually share what I'm proposing them to share?
- Should I do this as the company or as my personal brand?

To answer these questions, you'll need to get creative: creative in how you understand social media, creative in how you understand your company, and creative in how you understand your customers. Think of yourself as an international marketing executive trying to take a product and adapt it for use in another country. You would want to do some research on the demographics of the country, its history and language, and a whole list of other factors before you would be comfortable launching your product there, wouldn't you?

The same thing goes for social media marketing to different networks. If you were to attempt to start marketing on a new network you've never tried before, you would do best if you prepared yourself by studying the network, how it works, and how your message would fit in. This is where the *Shout in the Right Direction Social Media Culture Guide* comes in. To shout in the right direction, use these factors to understand the platform you're going to be using first. It's like a travel guide that helps you navigate all the different social platforms (they are like their own countries, you know).

So here is the *Shout in the Right Direction Social Media Culture Guide*.

Demographics
Who uses it?

Considering demographics as part of culture is the most traditional way to look at social marketing. Just like with any marketing message, giving consideration to who you're trying to reach is the best way to customize a message. When applying this approach to the social realm, there are a few twists that help you extend beyond the traditional sense of demographic (and psychographic) targeting.

In the strictest sense, you can try to consider the demographics of the user base of a particular platform. We've found that there are only a few cases where this is particularly useful (one of them being below), as most social media platforms are so large that there are enough people to carve out any niche you like. Facebook, for example, has such a broad demographic and adoption over so many different demographic areas that it almost isn't helpful (in our humble opinion) to try to consider the demographics of Facebook's user base when considering it for a campaign.

So are there cases in which user demographic data tells you something about what types of campaigns will be successful? Yes. For example, a as we're writing, Pinterest has a demographic of nearly 70 percent women, and half of the users have children.[1] With such a specific and defined base, you might gain some strategic advantages by doing a traditional evaluation of the demographics, if you're considering Pinterest as a venue for your campaign.

If you freeze up when thinking of the user demographic of a whole platform, it is sometimes helpful to bring your thoughts down to street level. If you're planning a specific marketing campaign and are looking at LinkedIn, for example, you might consider targeting a few LinkedIn groups (the collections of LinkedIn users who network through shared discussions, announcement, etc.) instead of the entire platform. In this case, your strategic decision-making process will be easier. When deciding whether or not to dedicate resources to making a presence in a group, it's a good exercise to decide if the group has people in it that you would like to connect with. The added social twist is that when you make this connection, you not only connect with the members of the group, but you also can potentially connect with the people whom they're connected to as well.

History and Shared Language
How do people talk on it, and what do people use it for?

Using the history and shared language of a platform to your advantage is all about capitalizing on how people are accustomed to doing things. This can work its magic in tons of different ways, but it's important to consider how your marketing effort fits into the context of what's been done in the past. There's something to be said about tapping into an existing habit or way of thinking to help "grease the wheels" and get your message to catch on.

---

1   *http://mashable.com/2012/02/25/pinterest-user-demographics/*

Twitter users have a huge shared vocabulary unique to the platform and this drives how Twitter users behave. For example, the "Follow Friday" (#FF) trend is ubiquitous across the platform: Users are accustomed to seeing and interacting with Follow Friday tweets and retweets. Learning Twitter's lingo is one of the first steps to starting any effort to connect on the platform, as the sharing methods (such as @ mentions and retweets) are fundamentally tied up in the language used to share it.

Learning the shared history also has another important benefit: You get to learn what has worked, what has crashed and burned, and worse, what hasn't made any sort of splash. Reddit is an example of a community whose purpose is to share the most relevant links across the web, but there are several factors that dictate what types of links do well and which don't. Since the users up- and down-vote pieces of content to determine how much it gets shared, studying and learning from the history of what's done well can help you position your content and social media efforts to encourage those up-votes.

Individual vs. Company vs. Group
Who does the connecting? Individuals, companies, or something else?

Unit emphasis has to do with *the identity of what is shared the easiest.* While it may seem confusing to think of a platform in this way, it's really just about this question: Who is sharing what, and under what name are they doing so? Let's illustrate this idea with a comparison.

LinkedIn is a platform with several competing acting units, all of which have differing levels of influence over LinkedIn users' behaviors. For example, the major "units" on LinkedIn are the individual, the company, and the group. Individuals have the opportunity to connect with other individuals, be a part of their own company, and follow other companies. In the same way, individuals can find community in "groups," while the groups have a different dynamic than do company units. Despite the fact that there are several different acting units, the "individual" is still the most prominent (again, in our humble opinion).

In this way, a campaign based on encouraging LinkedIn users to share with one another would be planned and implemented in a different way than a campaign leveraging a group or company following. Yet, knowing and accounting for the different units on a platform allows you to evaluate all of the possible avenues to promote your campaign.

Media Support
Can the platform share pictures, video, audio, and if so, how easily?

Media support deals with the types of media that spread best across a platform. When comparing media support, consider that a campaign that aims to spread photos through social media would likely work better on Facebook than on Twitter. The difference is because of media support.

Although Twitter has embraced photos in recent years, the support isn't as native as it is for Facebook. Many users on Twitter need to click on a tweet to see its associated photos, whereas on Facebook, the photos display in news feeds automatically. With this reduced action needed to interact with the campaign item, Facebook would likely be a better supporter of this campaign's promotion.

You can do similar analysis for video, streaming video, audio, podcasts, and even ease of linking to blog articles. If your campaign depends on some sort of media, you must consider the support and ease of sharing that media.

Communication Constraints
Do you have to get creative with your communication?

Communication constraints often have a profound effect on shaping how users behave on social platforms. Twitter is a prime example of this, since it limits the length of all communications to 140 characters. While you may look at this in the light of "what platform gives me the least amount of constraints to communications," it doesn't always have to be that way. As with any great design project, sometimes constraints drive creativity: Constrained platforms often have developed an interesting culture as people have figured out how to connect online inside of those same constraints.

On the other hand, constraints can be a bit of a nuisance for a campaign. LinkedIn is famous for limiting the amount of communication that promotes products in an effort to combat spam. For example, group managers on LinkedIn can send out only one e-mail announcement per week to their entire group. LinkedIn also puts restraints on the access to e-mail addresses for contacts in order to combat its users getting e-mail spam. While it does have a legitimate use to protect the users, this limitation can be a bit of a pain when trying to promote your business or campaign. So, when choosing your platform, do some trial runs to investigate the constraints on your communication. You can use this to either encourage yourself to choose another platform, or to help drive a creative way to communicate with your base despite the constraints (which can sometimes be more fun, and help bring your group together).

Sharing Dynamics
How exactly are things shared on the site?

Sharing dynamics are hugely important in a social media campaign—especially ones that bank on users to share your company's message as a part of promoting the campaign.

One strategy in evaluating a social media platform's sharing dynamics is to evaluate successful campaigns created by other businesses that you've encountered yourself. How did you find it? Did you as a user have to perform a conscious action to in order to share the item, or did it share passively as result of your doing something else (like pressing "Like" on Facebook)?

As part of your campaign, it's important to plan out all of the potential ways that users are going to share your campaign. In some cases, determining this calls for user testing: Observing people go through the motions that a user would go through to share your campaign. Conducting user testing can help you figure out what encourages more sharing.

In order to put this concept to a tangible example, let's adapt it to consider the sharing dynamics of a now-ubiquitous social sharing tool: the Facebook "Like" button. As using this button has exploded across the web, web developers, marketers, and users have adapted the button to work in a myriad of different ways—some of which are more beneficial than others. For instance, instead of the using "Like" button, consider a tool that allows users to post a status update or share a post on a friend's page. Encouraging one of these other sharing mechanisms would have different effects on your campaign's success, depending on your strategic goals.

Considering sharing dynamics can influence your strategic decisions and provide you with a different way of looking at things: Even a seemingly simple decision like putting a Facebook "Like" button on your site can be an opportunity for strategic advantage to marketers who take the time to consider the implications.

Intimacy
How personal do people get on the site?

Some social networks are more intimate than others. The level of intimacy on a social network is sometimes difficult to detect, but comparing different platforms can often describe how differences in intimacy can affect your social strategy.

Take a moment to imagine a real-life situation where some foresight and planning about the intimacy of a venue would have helped the poor protagonist of our story. A well-dressed man walks slowly up the sidewalk toward the door of his blind date. He rings the doorbell, and she answers the door dressed in a bright red dress and wearing a mysterious smile. The man invites her outside and down the sidewalk toward his car. Being a chivalrous gentleman, he opens the door of his car for his date and escorts her smoothly into her seat. After gently closing the car door to secure his date, he sprints quickly around the car to join her in the driver's seat. She flashes him an excited but nervous smile has he starts the car and begins to pull away toward their destination.

Having never been on a blind date before, the woman's nervousness about the date begins to fade and she begins to open up. Just as she begins to feel comfortable, the car makes a slight right turn in the parking lot of a McDonald's. Confused, she asks her date, "Are we turning around or something?" He replies, "Nope, we're here. We can split a value meal." Instantly, the excitement and mysterious smile melts off her face as she begins to silently curse the friends who set her up.

So what was wrong with our well-dressed (yet regrettably cheap) young protagonist? He failed to think properly about how his date would respond to the intimacy of the venue of his planned date. Planning social media is a lot like planning a date (first or otherwise). Certain situations require a certain level of social comfort to be effective. When you're planning out a social media strategy for your company, really try to step into the shoes of your customers who are going to share your message on your behalf. How intimate of a setting is required to get the message across?

The effect of this is extremely profound, based on what you're promoting, what your brand's image is, and what your customers expect to share about their experience. For example, Facebook is much more intimate than a professional network like LinkedIn. If your company is one whose service is highly personal (such as a restaurant), the intimacy of the social network you're planning to market on will have an effect on your marketing success. Though a person may be excited to share a great lunch experience on Facebook with their personal friends, that same person may not be motivated to share that information on LinkedIn with their professional colleagues.

Conversely, if your brand is highly professional (and associated with business-to-business services, for example) you may have more success in getting your customers to talk about you on LinkedIn. Those same customers may not want to bother their personal friends on Facebook with business talk.

Adoption and Consistent Use
How many people use it, and how often?

Everyone in business is familiar with risk: We all constantly put time and resources into different marketing and advertising. Every time you put time and money into a marketing effort (even social media marketing that may be free to use), you're taking a risk that you may or may not be able to recoup that time and money in more sales. Attempting to balance the risk of spending time with the potential benefit of getting more sales is your job as the "chooser of the marketing strategy."

One of the factors that can help you balance this risk is to consider if the platform you're considering has "caught on," and how often your target audience uses the platform. The ideal platform will have high adoption by your target audience. A high level of adoption is strategically helpful for a couple of reasons.

Firstly, it increases the likelihood that a particular potential customer will have an account on that platform in the first place (they can't connect with you if they aren't there themselves). Secondly, a high level of adoption can give you some additional security that the platform will be around for a while. The social media world is very fickle: what is today's hot website can be tomorrow's MySpace. This is part of the risk that we take as social media managers: even if we spend months and months building a presence on a social media site, it can still implode.

That being said, you need to assess the different social media platforms out there and determine which one, if any, is suitable for you to spend your limited time on. When you're thinking about the landscape of social media sites, we've found it useful to lump social sites into two categories.

The Safe Mainstream

Highly mainstream social media sites have thoroughly made their way into general use, and have a high level of general public name recognition. Currently, platforms that we consider to be "safe and mainstream" are Facebook, Twitter, LinkedIn, YouTube, and a few others.

The highly mainstream social media sites have the benefit of the high penetration into the general population, and generally high level of engagement of the registered users (though both of these factors vary greatly by site). Choosing to set up a presence on these sites is usually a safe bet, though the sheer number of people on the site makes competition for attention intense.

Just like the saying "no one ever gets fired for buying IBM," no social media manager ever gets fired for setting up shop on these main networks. While it's true that the platforms are tried and true, there usually isn't anything particularly innovative about being there.

The Unsettled Newcomers

With the rate at which new social media sites have been launched, most of us are constantly bombarded with decisions of whether or not to establish a presence on new platforms. Though it's often tempting to try to be everywhere, putting up an account on every new platform can be a recipe for disaster for small businesses. On one hand, creating too many social profiles can be distracting to manage, and can split the focus and limited resources that might be better spent concentrated on a small number of profiles. Secondly, the future of many newcomer social platforms is not clear. For example, even if a site is experiencing a meteoric rise in popularity, there is no telling if it will be able to sustain that level of growth. Careful research is necessary when considering a newcomer platform, as its adoption is likely not equal across demographics: If you're going to spend time there, you should make sure your target audience is there first.

That being said, there is some benefit to staking your claim in an unsettled space; after all, it's wide open to colonize. Most new platforms have not yet established their cultural norms or their major players. Significant opportunities are available to be the first to establish a presence in a new area, but only if the growth of the platform continues as expected.

Choosing platforms to focus on can be a balancing act. On one hand, you'll want to have a presence everywhere your customers are, but on the other hand your limited time and resources may cause you to stretch yourself too thin if you try to be everywhere at once. Whatever your marketing case, your choice of platform should be based on your specific needs. A single great idea can trump generic conventional wisdom. If you find a niche social website growing in your specific customer base, it may be worthwhile to break your typical focus and incorporate a riskier marketing channel into the mix. It all depends on where your customers are, so think this through and make informed choices.

How to Put the Social Media Culture Guide into Practice

Hopefully, the Social Media Culture Guide has given you some perspective on how to approach social media culture. It can serve as a base point for brainstorming, strategic planning, and day-to-day activity planning.

At the end of the day though, make sure you're pushing yourself to just try something.

Research and planning is very important, don't get us wrong. But we have seen cases in the past where "research paralysis" has postponed smart and capable businesspeople from putting their ideas into action for months at a time.

As you're putting together your plan, use the Social Media Culture Guide to make it the best plan you can, but do your best to put something (anything) into action as soon as you can. You'll get much more knowledge and direction from putting something out there quickly than you would planning for an extended period of time, so force yourself to plan and act quickly.

If you go through this process, you'll have a social media marketing plan that shouts in the right direction in no time!

18

Keeping a List: How Small Companies Use Databases to Market Online

Building a database is an essential part of creating a long-term business strategy. Essentially, it consists of two parts, which require systems to be designed to make them more efficient: list-building systems, and to help you focus your plan and execute your communications to the people in your database. In this chapter, we discuss two different approaches to list building that serve different purposes: customer relationship management (CRM) systems and e-mail newsletter lists.

Why have two systems? Because it's best to have two different approaches to list building. Using e-mail marketing involves getting as large of a list of names as possible for mass messaging to the entire group. When using e-mail marketing, the biggest, most relevant database wins. This mass-marketing approach is great for putting yourself into constant contact with anyone who may have any sort of interest in your business: the general public, customers, referral partners, and everyone else who's relevant. CRM takes a different approach: instead of managing mass messaging, CRM systems help optimize the process of delegating and tracking one-to-one messages with sales prospects.

In this way, you can think of the databases as having two different functions: E-mail marketing is more for getting company messages and information out there, whereas CRM is better for sales and optimizing those individual communications. Just as you can't run a business without both sales and marketing, using both e-mail marketing databases and customer relationship-management sales databases will help you optimize both of those processes so you're more efficient and effective.

E-mail Newsletter Systems

Notable providers (Constant Contact, Mailchimp, Aweber):

When considering e-mail newsletters, your general approach should be to generate a list of potential customers who have "opted in" to receive e-mails from you. As with building a social media brand, the best way to approach this is to brand your e-mail marketing system so that it provides value to the customer. You can make it both valuable to sign up for the list, and valuable to remain on the list.

For example:

Your company sells widgets, and you want to entice your potential widget-using customers to sign up for your e-mail list. Two challenges arise: How to entice them on to the list, and how to keep them engaged once you have them on the list. Only after settling these two issues can you face the third fundamental task of e-mail marketing: to intrigue people down the sales funnel.

Being a savvy marketer yourself, you know that the best way to do this is to add value. Working with your team, you create a set of white papers detailing what widget-buyers need to know when considering their next widget-production contract. You contact your web people to have your e-mail sign-up system integrated into your website, but with an incentive. You advertise on the site that the site visitor can get this amazingly useful and valuable white paper by simply entering their name and e-mail address. Simple as that!

Every business has to educate its customers as a part of the sales process. Your customers need to understand the services you offer before they will be comfortable making a buying decision. E-mail marketing is a fantastic tool to help educate customers about complicated services over time. Your customers won't admit how little they understand about the ways your services work: it's your job to make sure they understand. Sending them a huge amount of information all at once isn't always effective, because most people won't retain everything they read. But, they *will* remember pertinent information that's given to them in small bits over time. As long as you keep your content engaging and useful, you can think of your e-mail list as your education channel for your customers: You would be amazed how much your satisfied customers want to refer out your services to others, but don't know enough about what you offer to know how to refer you well. Using e-mail to provide them with a slow and constant "drip campaign" will help them learn more about your services and be more comfortable referring you—and using your services themselves.

Once the sign-up system is in place, it's time to turn attention to what exactly to send to the people on your list. Once again, this comes down to value. Before you send out any e-mail to your list, ask yourself if you would find this particular e-mail valuable if you were your customer. If it sounds like spam, don't send it! You'll just be hurting your future chances for getting sales from your list.

Opt-In E-mail Newsletter Systems

When the CAN-SPAM Act passed, critics argued that it didn't go far enough to stop spam, as the bill does not *actually* stop businesses from sending unsolicited commercial e-mail. It only banned the most egregious of e-mail abuses. Because of this, though it may technically be *legal* to send out a spammy unsolicited e-mail, you may be hard-pressed to find a provider that will allow you to do so.

Here's why.
When we log in to our Gmail accounts in the morning, we get the pleasure of seeing an inbox free of spam (for the most part). That's because

Gmail filters spam e-mails out of inboxes automatically. Think about that. Gmail's algorithms make a decision about an e-mail's spammyness before it even reaches an inbox. As it turns out, almost every e-mail provider out there filters inboxes for spam. When you're a marketer trying to get your e-mails to customers, the art of "e-mail deliverability" helps you make sure that your e-mail ends up in an inbox and not a spam box.

The way we get around the spam filter is by pledging ourselves to high standards of e-mail integrity: the opt-in only e-mail list.

When you use an e-mail list provider (such as Constant Contact, Mailchimp, Aweber, Emma, MadMimi, etc.), you get lots of e-mail marketing goodies. They help you keep your list up to date, automatically add new subscribers, remove subscribers that want to unsubscribe, and track all kinds of data related to your list. These perks are great! When you work with a good provider, you will find that nearly all of your e-mails get delivered to the inbox. They will get delivered much more often than if you sent them out on your own (from your own e-mail account).

Why is this you ask? It's because they promise to police their users.

When you use an e-mail list provider, you promise the provider only to e-mail people who have "opted in" to receive e-mails from you. Think about that. They only allow you to e-mail people who have specifically asked to receive e-mail from you. And your e-mail list provider has a lot to lose if it fails to police you well enough. To make a long story short, your e-mail provider will be monitoring your e-mail activity to ensure that the people to whom you're sending out e-mails *actually expect* to get e-mails from you.

Yes, this seems restrictive, but it's helpful to think of it as a blessing. Most creative people will tell you that constraints help drive innovation. When you're only sending to people who have opted in to your list, most everyone on the list *actually wants to hear from you*. When you send out a message, people are waiting and ready to read what you have to say.

Constraining the focus of your e-mail marketing audience helps you to shout in the right direction. And focusing your e-mail marketing strategy should be highly related to your business strategy. Who are you trying to reach? What defines them? What are the interested in? What do they find valuable? What is their level of knowledge of what you do? Are they novices or do they have expertise? Answering these types of questions will help you narrow down your audience. The more you target your e-mail subscribers, the better you will be able to give them value. When they're deciding if they're going to open and read your newsletter along with all the other e-mails in their inboxes in the morning, having a good reputation for providing valuable content is crucial.

The actual content of what you send is up to you to experiment with. When you're trying to judge how effective your e-mails are, you can pay attention to a few key metrics: open rate and click rate. These two metrics detail how often your audience opens your e-mails, and subsequently how often they click on a link in an opened e-mail. When you're trying to drive traffic to your site, optimizing both of these metrics will increase your sales. The open rate you can expect for your e-mails varies widely by industry (and by how engaged your e-mail list members are).

Using e-mail marketing is a strategy that grows over time. As with many forms of marketing, it is largely a numbers game. Though it might not seem like you're getting a good return when starting your list with a few hundred people, in a few years (with perseverance) you'll thank yourself when you can publish a single newsletter that reaches thousands of people at once. Using an e-mail list (like most forms of Internet marketing) is a great way to amplify and direct your voice. Just by virtue of keeping up your consistency, your list will keep growing.

Remember: e-mail marketing is all about value. Since your list will opt-in only, customers aren't forced to be on it: and it's easy as pie for them to unsubscribe or report you for sending spam. Provide value in your sign-up system and with every e-mail you send, and your list will continue to grow. Content is everything!

Segmentation

When trying to create the perfect piece of content for every person on your list, e-mail newsletter list tools offer a particular advantage: segmentation. With most social media channels, you send out the same message to everyone (for the most part); that's not so with e-mail lists. You can segment a single e-mail list into multiple groups, or even have different lists for different purposes.

It may seem like it's just more work for you (which, in some senses it is) to have multiple segments making up your e-mail list: but we promise you, taking advantage of this option is a good idea. Think about all the people you interact with. Do you talk to them differently? Of course you do. Just the simple fact of if someone is already a customer or not will affect how you talk to them.

Here are some groups that you may consider segmenting:
- Current customers
- Potential customers
- Past customers
- Partners and other people who recommend you but don't buy from you.
- Blog subscribers
- Even more creative segments, such as:

    o People who signed up on your website and who are interested in a particular topic
    o People whose contact information you got from trade shows
    o Potential customers who have something in common, such as a location or market segment (like Minnesota business owners, or secretaries in the Twin Cities area who would use your product in a specific way).

Now, you don't need to make this many segments. The goal is to spend a little time setting up a system that will help you in the future. Each group of contacts will respond to a different message and a different approach. Defining these segments therefore helps you focus your efforts so you're reaching the right people, the right way.

Once you define the segments that are relevant to your business, you can put together general goals for each type of person and how they might interact with your e-mail list. For example, you might have a set of goals like this that governs all your e-mail communications:

1. Developing relationships with new prospects and bringing prospects down the marketing funnel.
2. Maintaining contact with current and past clients, encouraging them to purchase again, and making sure they're still happy with your service.
3. Identifying, educating, and keeping in contact with referral partners who offer your services to their own clients.

Making a System and Defining How Your Funnel Works for Different Groups

Segmenting your e-mail list will not only help you improve your e-mail-list communications, but it can also force you to tailor you entire messaging and business offerings more closely to different groups of people. Done effectively, every qualified[1] person you meet will fit into one of the specific areas: prospect, client, or referral partner. Designing intelligent (and manageable) segments will help you quickly triage any potential prospect into a relationship-building process.

In this way, e-mail marketing can be the first part of your sales funnel if you choose to set your process up that way. After defining segments for your e-mail list, you can then create a drip marketing e-mail campaign designed to bring each of the segments to the next level of engagement with your company. If you have a prospects segment, one approach could be to send them occasional content they would find useful, inspiring, or interesting. Taking such a "soft sell" approach will build trust with the people on your list, and give them additional opportunities to see your brand name.[2]

1   *When you develop your marketing process, you only want to consider people who are qualified to use your services. If they're not in your market (or aren't reasonably going to be in your market in the future), don't spend your time on them, but move on.*
2   *One of the nice things about e-mail marketing is that even subscribers who don't open your e-mail will see your address come across their inbox. When you ask them in*

Lots of e-mail-list builders swear by different strategies to get your list to convert to customers, and you may want to try lots of different strategies with people on your own list. For example, some newsletter marketers never have any hard sales in their e-mail (and solely send out content that promotes brand awareness and trust) while others are masters of the hard call to action, crafting each e-mail to be a specific action-ready offer. Whatever path you choose, just consider balancing the two extremes of value and sales. The last thing you want is for your e-mail subscribers to get turned off by e-mail consisting solely of a cheap "buy from me" pleas. As long as you discipline yourself to make sure you're not spamming, your prospects will thank you (and become more loyal).

If you have more segments than just a prospects segment (such as, say, current clients and referral partners segments), consider taking a different approach. The beauty of segmenting and targeting your list is that you get to customize your messages specifically for specific segments. To do that with current customers, for example, just answer the question, "What do my current clients want to hear?" Your current clients may not need to have the "soft sell," because they're already sold on one product or another. But they may be interested in up-sell deals, value-added resources specifically for them, new product offerings, event notifications, etc. If you maintain a list of referral partners, that list is an entirely different animal altogether, because the person receiving the message isn't the person buying the product, but the person selling the product. Messaging that educates your referral partners about your product offerings and specific ideas for referring you will play well with them.

You can do this with your general business audiences as well. Think up a process for every group of qualified people you encounter. What's the next step with each one? Coming up with a customized pitch for every person is a very involved and often wasteful process. By developing a standardized system, you can easily put every qualified person you meet through a pre-defined process that contributes to your company's strategic goals.

---

person, they'll tell you, "Of course I read your e-mails," while they're thinking, "I read them . . . as I'm deleting them." But they're still reading them . . . All the more reason to have a great subject line.

Developing this standardized process is at the core of shouting in the right direction. Your marketing process is what helps you scale your marketing approach and messaging. There's only so much a single person (or a single team) can do in a day; slicing your market up into segments helps you to better target your communications and become more efficient. Shouting in the right direction means getting to know your customers better by understanding their needs. It means finding out exactly who should be hearing which of your messages, so you can leverage your time by spending it only where it will produce the best results. It means creating a process that helps you eliminate wasted effort. It means growing the power of your voice and influence in your target area.

19

Driving Traffic: Using Search Optimization and Content

How do you know if you exist? Fifteenth-century French philosopher René Descartes would tell you that the very fact that you are able to contemplate your own existence proves that you exist (famously stating, "I think, therefore I am"). Though neither of us is always convinced of our own existence, we tend to take a simpler approach to "existence" when talking about the web.

On the Internet, you only exist if Google[1] knows about you.

With the astounding number of people who use search engines to find information, one of the keys to being relevant in the digital age is figuring out how to capture some of that traffic to your own website. Luckily, there's a whole suite of things you can do to bring in this traffic. Welcome to the world of search engine optimization (SEO).

---

1   *In principle, we're talking about all the major search engines. But for the sake of a Twitter-sized quote, we left them out.*

Search Engine Optimization

At its core, SEO is like any other process of optimization: it involves implementing a process of constant improvement. It involves the resource investment daily activities such as blog writing and research, and also systems and technology like websites and hosting. It is a multidisciplinary process, with its sphere encompassing website copywriters, developers, and designers.

To make matters harder on businesses, there's a whole swath of SEO mythology out there on the Internet. These SEO-ranking folk tales contain a range of SEO tips, tricks, and advice, not all of it relevant, hardly any of it easy to understand, and much of it hurtful if not followed correctly and ethically. With all of the different types of advice out there, it's difficult to choose which ones to follow (or even to keep track of the sheer volume of different opinions). Even for those in the marketing profession, keeping on top of all the changes in SEO best practice is daunting.

There is a way to proceed, though. Despite all the constantly changing advice, we've found that you only need to keep in mind two guiding principles to bring your website onto the path to SEO success: think like Google, and remember to be human. Using these two rules of thumb will set you on the path toward making an impact on your rankings without having to spend hours and hours delving into the seedy depths of the murky world of SEO best practice world.

How to Think like Google

You can effectively make 90 percent of your SEO decisions by simply putting yourself in Google's shoes. Imagine for a moment that you are a product manager at Google. Your job is to make sure that visitors to Google have a good experience-specifically that users receive relevant, useful results to whatever they search for. You'd likely be partial, then, to sending users to resources that have established authority on the topic the user is searching for. If a website has been around for a long time, and is referenced by other websites of authority, you would likely be more convinced that the website will provide good information to your user.

All you have to do to make good SEO decisions is to put yourself in Google's shoes in that way. Google likes to rank websites that provide relevant and authoritative content to its users. Along the way, here are some of the broad areas to consider when trying to entice Google to rank your pages.

SEO Authority and Offsite Optimization

Google attempts to assess how authoritative your site is on any topic you're attempting to rank for. Any time we find a really great resource on the Internet somewhere, what do we often do? We might write blogs article about it, or link to it on our resources pages on our websites, or share it on social media, or all of the above. You want to be a resource that others rely on and talk about in this way. Google takes all of these cues in deciding if a site has authority on the web; if other people of authority cite or point to your website consistently, Google may determine that your site is authoritative.

As you build authority, pay special attention to the amount of inbound links pointing to your website: the more valid links you have from other authoritative websites, the more Google will consider your site to be an authority on your topic.

SEO Technical Side

Apart from the link-building side of SEO, there is another side that is largely under your control: the side that has to do with technical aspects of your website. Again, imagine that you work for Google: you would want to send users to websites that load quickly, don't have errors, don't have pages under construction, and a whole host of other techy things.

Most of us aren't web designers and developers; if this includes you, you should check with your web person to make sure your website is up to spec and technical things on your website aren't hurting your rankings.

SEO Creative Side

Sometimes, when people write content with an eye for SEO, they focus solely on making Google's algorithms happy. Content written in this way is never fun to read, and it's usually not very compelling. We affectionately call content like this "SEO vomit."

You know when you're reading a page or article on a site with SEO vomit. They're the sites that have added five hundred tags to the blog article in an effort to bring in traffic from every corner of Google. They're the ones that add those subtle word insertions like "Minneapolis" and "social media consultant" into the blog article text.

Don't forget: You might have an awesome SEO strategy that tells you to stuff your article full of keywords, but actual humans have to read (and like) your article for you to get any results.

As marketing consultants, we never discount the value of SEO in bringing in traffic. But it is extremely important to balance the traffic generation potential of SEO with actually providing readable and engaging content for the readers that arrive at your site.

It doesn't matter how much traffic you get to your blog if all your articles are keyword-stuffed SEO vomit. As it turns out, Google and other search engines have begun to wise up to keyword stuffing in recent algorithm updates. Just another reason to write for humans first: SEO will come if you focus on writing good content.

There is, of course, more to the story.

Hopefully this section on SEO has given you some of the basics of how to understand and think about SEO strategy. Keep in mind that search engine optimization is a very complex topic with algorithms and best practices constantly changing. If you keep in mind that search engines just want you to put out good stuff for their readers, you won't go wrong, but if you want to embark on a serious SEO strategy, you'll need to do some more reading and research.

Content Marketing

Now, it's time to execute. One of the most effective ways to go about leveraging your keyword list to your advantage is to use a content marketing approach. Content marketing is all about attracting website visitors and client leads by creating content. Here are some reasons why content marketing is so successful:

It fills a consumer need:

When you create content that fulfills customers' needs, by definition you create something of value for your customers. You're creating value. Effective content helps build a relationship with your current and potential customers by giving them information that they want.

It makes search engines love you:

Content marketing is one of the most effective ways to implement your search engine marketing keyword list. When people search for information about your niche or industry, the more content you have in the search engine indexes on that topic, the more traffic and lead opportunities your website receives.

It makes you human and personable:

It's tough to convey your personality on the Internet. It's difficult to actually get to know people (or, God forbid, bring them to trust you). When you publish writing to provide value to your customers, you connect more effectively to them. It gives your audience a way to actually see who you are. You can talk to only so many people person to person; the more of yourself that you put on the web, the more opportunity people have to understand your voice, your passions, and why you do what you do. People don't simply care what you do, they care why you do it. Ultimately, your website content is to make your company money, but it's good to connect with people on a non-business level, too. You are really trying to get to know people. People do business with those whom they know, like, and trust. When they read your content, you connect on those levels.

It lets people know how much you know about your topic:

When you publish content about your industry and niche, your potential customers are able to get a preview of what they'll receive from you as actual customers. They are able to really understand your depth of knowledge, which is a great way to build trust. And publishing your knowledge gives you a chance to give back to your industry while establishing yourself as a leader.

People naturally share good content on the Internet:

Appeal to people's desire to share good information with other people that they know by shaping your content so it's about more than just your brand. When you make something useful, people will share. People in your market will tell others, and others will tweet, like, and reblog your best content, helping to spread it throughout the web.

Blogging

Blogging is great. It's that simple. Just like what the printing press (Gutenberg), public library (Benjamin Franklin), and the Internet (Al Gore[2]) did for the sharing of knowledge, blogging has lowered the barriers to accessing and publishing information. Never before has it been easier for anyone with a voice to get his or her information out to the world. This trend is true in business as well; spreading messages online isn't limited to huge companies any more. Small- and medium-size companies can get online and market with the best of 'em.

The real point of a blog:

You may wonder why, exactly, blogs have exploded in popularity so quickly. Blogging has become so pervasive for good reason. A well-executed blog has the ability to positively impact several areas of your business. To sum up why you should consider adding a blog to your marketing rotation:

---

2   *Don't you just love it how one mis-paraphrase can stick with you forever? But we digress.*

- Blog articles are easy to share on social media.
- Regularly contributing to a blog gives you an opportunity to share your company's expertise with potential customers.
- When you write about your expertise, you learn more about it (seriously, it happens).
- Blog articles help you contribute to the whole of knowledge in your area of expertise.
- Constant updates keep your customers coming back to your site.
- Sending out blog articles through e-mail keeps your company and brand on the top of your customers' minds.
- Writing blog articles helps bring in more search traffic to your website (if you do it right).
- A blog can serve LOADS of different purposes: official communication, content-rich training articles, executive messaging, community development, and the list goes on.
- Writing allows you to bring outsiders inside to your company: they can see your culture, your ideas, and how you work.
- Blogs support all kinds of great media: photos, videos, podcasts, white papers, and more.

Choose a scope: What is your blog about? This is the most important thing to determine when you are branding your blog. It's very easy to get sidetracked and deviate from your scope (especially when people want to write guest articles, and they want to write about what *they're* interested in). When choosing your blog's scope, consider these factors:

- *Your target demographic:* What are they interested in? What types of content do they consume?
- *Your competition:* How many different blogs are on your topic in your industry? Can you find a niche that's not as competitive?
- *Your authors:* Who is going to write the blog posts? Do they have the expertise to write on the topic you've determined to be your blog's focus?

Then there's your breadth of scope. Should it be wide or narrow? With a wide scope, you may attract more potential readers, but you may become less relevant as there's more competition. Narrow scopes offer less competition and more relevance, but you may have fewer people potentially interested in your topic. No matter which way you go, remember: You can easily become the *definitive expert in your niche,* and you'll be surprised how big your niche actually can get. If you blog, you'll be more engaged.

Choose your frequency of blogging and stick to it:

Just as with all of your other digital marketing platforms, it's important to be consistent in your blogging. When you create your comprehensive communications editorial calendar, plan out how often you're going to release a blog post, and stick to it. If you don't have time to blog, hire someone to help, but do whatever you can to make sure your blog doesn't go stale—if you want it to perform well for you. A reasonable goal when you're starting out is to blog weekly, but you'll get even more benefit from the blog if you end up blogging daily (especially, for example, if you have a product that is digital, and your relationship with a large audience is important).

Compose amazing articles:

Start with a clearly defined idea and title. The most important part of the post is the title. Make sure to choose a title that is interesting, catchy, and easily coverable in about 350 to 550 words. If you use your blog to generate company website traffic, the title is of special importance. It heavily influences how search engines index your post. Try to write blog posts that address common questions or issues that potential customers might research by searching on Google.

Write a clear introduction paragraph. Whatever your article topic is, it will seem more important if you take some time to introduce it. Your readers will want to know the context of your article, who the article is meant for, and why they should continue reading it. A good introduction addresses all three of these. It doesn't have to be more than a paragraph or two: just make sure the reader knows what he or she is getting into.

Make your posts easy to skim. Online readers have notoriously short attention spans. When a web user comes upon a blog post, he or she wants to know right away if it is worth reading. Make it easy for your readers.

Keep your paragraphs short (bite-sized text s easier to read). Make your writing concise and to the point. Above all, use bold text and subheads to break up your posts. Your reader should be able to summarize your article by reading only the bold text.

Always include interesting media. Let's face it: text can be boring. Make sure to jazz up every post with at least one image or video. The easiest thing you can do is upload your own images (if you have any you would like to share). If you don't have any publication-worthy images of your own, you can purchase an image for use on your blog from a stock photography website.

Include a call to action at the end. What do you want your readers to do after they read your post? Do you want them to read other related posts? Do you want them to check out a website? Do you want them to follow you on social media sites? Whatever it is you want them to do, ask it outright at the end of the post. This encourages maximum compliance.

Don't worry; you won't give it all away:

Resist the urge to think that you're giving away proprietary information. Yes, you should use good judgment about whether or not you should publish your ultrasecret stuff, but try to also embrace the mentality that giving away things of value for free is a good thing. Sharing knowledge freely is how you will get the best value and the most loyal readership. If you're concerned about sharing too much and giving away the farm, just use your expertise to comment on industry trends.

Shout in the right direction by focusing on your audience and your goals, while blogging:

Blogging is a highly creative endeavor. For seasoned bloggers, inspiration for writing their regular blog articles comes from deep inside, and is as a reflection of what's meaningful to them. When blogging for business, though, we must always remember our audiences. Many newer bloggers focus more on what they have inside to share that what their customers need or want. Those who blog for marketing purposes soon learn that their blog is less about what they have to share, and more about what their audience yearns for.

As you're blogging, remember your purpose. When you set out on your blogging effort, did you create goals? Did you want people to contact you for business as a result of your blog? Sign up for your newsletter list? Follow you on Twitter? If you blog with your audience in mind, you will be more successful in encouraging them to come into your community, or approach you for business. In our experience, it's these types of goal conversions that keep bloggers going: it's much easier to keep up the consistency when the rewards come in.

20

How to Measure (Things That Are Actually Meaningful)

Getting concrete numbers on your marketing activities helps you to improve them. As self-described "social ecologist" Peter Drucker has said, "What gets measured gets managed." Just from getting data on something, we humans improve it. We just do.

That's what this chapter is about: Using analytics dashboards and reporting to measure your results, because knowing your results is an integral part to shouting in the right direction. How are you supposed to know if you are targeting and amplifying well if you don't measure? In this section, we go over the relevant tools that you should know about to measure easily and effectively.

Google Analytics

Google Analytics is a free platform for analyzing your website traffic. For marketing purposes, it can provide insight into critical metrics about your online marketing performance. In essence, it's your eyes directly into your website's traffic. It gives you so much information about your website visitors that it's almost creepy. Really.

You can tell which of your marketing initiatives give you the most traffic, how often your traffic converts to a submitted lead (such as someone filling out a web contact form), where your users get lost most on the way to conversion, and many technical details about your followers (like their computer and Internet connection statistics).

Individual Insights

Google Analytics has so many different metrics about your website visitors that it can be difficult to choose which to look at, much less which ones to act on. Over time, we've learned to focus on only the metrics that will help us make decisions about how our businesses run (to avoid the plague of obsessive stat-checking; we know you know what we're talking about).

Here are some of the things you can check on Google Analytics, and the rationale for caring about it:

1. Your general website traffic – to assess your general website marketing effectiveness.
2. Geographically where your traffic is coming from – if your business is local, you'll want to know where you're getting traction.
3. Traffic by page – find out what your most popular content is, so you can do more of it.
4. Traffic sources – the sources of your traffic can tell you several things:

    a. How important search engine marketing is to your business.
    b. If an online advertisement you're paying for is actually sending traffic to your site.
    c. How many people are typing in your website URL directly without being referred from anywhere else.
    d. Which one of your social media channels sends the most traffic to your website.

Those are the most common types of analyses that we recommend that people perform on their web traffic.

Connect with Conversions

What exactly is a conversion?

Conversion (n): In internet marketing, the **conversion rate** is the proportion of visitors to a website who take action.

Essentially, conversions are the magical outcome of good website marketing work. They're how you know you're successful in your efforts. And Google Analytics can help you measure them. The conversion goals you pick out as important may be different than what others would choose. You may want to track how many people submit a contact form, subscribe to your newsletter, follow you on social media, leave a comment, etc. Think carefully about your goals, and use Google Analytics to help you further those goals.

The Funnel: How Website Visitors Become Profit

One of the most common issues with social media is that most businesses have trouble measuring their effectiveness on the web. One of the ways to add measurable metrics to your strategy is to consider your business's website traffic conversion funnel.

Here's how it works:
1. Website visitors–of your website visitors, a certain percentage will convert to becoming leads or contacts. This is the *conversion rate*.
2. Leads–of your web-generated leads, a certain percentage of those will close in your sales process. This is the *close rate*.
3. Closed sales–of your closed sales, each generates profit (hopefully). For the purposes of this discussion, we will consider the *average profit per customer*.

An example calculation:
1. In a particular month, a business receives 5,000 website visitors. Over this time, the business realized a 1.5% conversion rate, generating 75 leads for its sales team.

2. Of these 75 generated leads, the sales team was able to close 40%, generating 30 closed sales.
3. The 30 closed sales generate, on average, $300 profit for the business, yielding $9,000 in profit for the business that month.

With data like that, a business can make powerful calculations and measurements of its efforts. You can see how an effect on your website traffic can affect the company's bottom line through web-generated leads (or the equivalent for your business).

Social Analytics Data
(Getting Info from Each Social Media Platform)

In addition to your website generating information and data, each of the social media profiles can provide some information about how your business's marketing is going. Again, just as with Google Analytics, social media platforms (and third-party systems) can provide a never-ending deluge of metrics and measurements for your marketing. In a theoretical sense, most people love being able to measure and quantify nearly every available metric. But in a practical sense, the sheer volume of numbers can provide a barrier to analyzing, interpreting, and implementing changes from it. For this reason, we recommend pulling together a small set of key metrics that are highly relevant to your business and marketing plan, checking them regularly, and checking all the other metrics "every once in a while."

Some things you may choose to measure are:
- Followers (page likes, followers, subscribers, etc.)
- Applause (likes, favorites, +1's, etc.)
- Amplification (shares, retweets, repins, etc.)
- Website traffic from each platform
- Leads generated by original referral from each platform

Some platforms will give you more detailed information, which can be useful to know as well. Facebook's Insights platform, for example, provides in-depth information as to the age and gender of your Facebook community, as well as engagement data on a post-by-post basis.

The name of the game is to create a measurement plan that you can live with. Yes, in a perfect world it would be great to know absolutely everything, but small businesses with limited resources are constantly pressured to balance the potential business improvements that come along with analytics and measurement with the time and money needed to create, interpret, and implement on the reports.

These are the Tools You Need to Shout in the Right Direcction

In this section, we've discussed a broad overview of the tools and platforms you will want to be familiar with as you navigate the social media world. It's our mission to bring you the practical tools you need so you can effectively shout in the right direction with your business by targeting your audience and amplifying your voice on the web.

Armed with the knowledge of each of the platforms, and some of the quirks and features of each, you should be well positioned to choose which of these you would like to add to your company's arsenal.

Choosing which platforms to include in your strategy has traditionally been all of what people think when they envision "social media strategy." And it's true that choosing the right platform is important to do well. But it's not the end of the story.

Part III – Creative:

Don't let thinking too much about technology and platforms get in the way of being really creative.

In this book, we've talked a lot about strategy and tools, and how understanding these aspects of the marketing plan is crucially important for understanding your business's marketing plan. Now we want you to put away that side of your brain. Put away the side of your brain that thinks about analytics, tools, and technology; it's time to get creative.

One of the common pitfalls about small business marketing is that marketers spend so much creative energy figuring out their websites, their e-mail newsletter systems, and their social media management systems (along with a million other tech-related things) that they don't leave themselves any creative bandwidth to make great messages. What good is having an e-mail list if the e-mails that you send to your target audience are trite and superficial? What good is a website with whiz-bang technology and animation if visitors can't easily understand what your business does? It probably isn't shocking that it doesn't do much good at all.

That's why we talk about getting creative. So far in *Shout in the Right Direction* we've discussed planning and tools. These provide the framework and the vehicles to get your message out into the world. But how, exactly, does one come up with that message? Your message is everything from your brand name, to your website copy, to the messages that you send out on social media. It's how you talk to your clients, and how you conduct yourself in networking situations, both online and off. All of these situations are places in which you have an opportunity to make an impression that can influence someone's perception about your business. Your potential clients don't care how much time you spent setting up your website: when they visit your site, they experience your message. Make sure that what they see when they get there rewards them for taking three minutes to learn more about you.

If you feel daunted by creating great messaging, don't worry: you're not alone. Once during a consult with a client, we were on the verge of implementing a digital marketing strategy on a scale that she had never done with her business before. The pressure of coming up with the best messaging and content was a bit overwhelming for her, leading her to ask, "What if I can't do it? What if I fail?"

For this particular client, her business meant more to her than just money: it was about helping people. We replied to her, "Don't worry. It's JUST your life's calling, isn't it? You'll find a way to make it work."

As you're going through this section, dig deep into your "why." Why is it that you're in business? Why do you get up to go work every day? Starting with your "why" will help you craft a message that none of your prospects can resist.

21

The Three Types of Social Media Actions

When it comes to social media, many business owners are overwhelmed by the sheer number of things that they can possibly do. In many cases, you can publish nearly any message your brain can come up with! On top of that, you can do this as many times a day as you please; and this is not the best situation for people who also want to run a business during that day.

The solution to this problem is to convey your messages through activities that have the highest value to your business. When it comes to the web, that often means making sure absolutely everything you're doing has a reasonable relation to one of your strategic business goals.

If you're not careful, you can easily get sucked into social media. We're sure you've experienced this. For your strategic pleasure, we've come up with three types of "social media actions" to help you focus your marketing plans on three broad types that have business value (we call these "Social Media Modes"). The three different types of social media actions are "broadcast mode," "campaign mode," and "one-to-one mode." Each of them has its own different style, different purpose, and a different way that it can be used to bring value to your business.

Because it is so easy to waste time on social media, try using these three social media modes to help direct your strategy for every activity you do online. That way, you'll never be spending your time on anything without a clear path to creating value for the business.

Let's look at each of these modes in more depth.

The Broadcast Mode

What it is: The "day in, day out" mode.

What it's good for: Helping you be consistent; putting valuable content out on the web.

The key tool for this mode: Editorial calendar.

The goal: Building the intangible "brand awareness" and acting on "serendipitous events."

How you know you're successful: Building "momentum," and growth of following.

Broadcast mode is what most people think of when they think of social media: the act of putting out messaging that your audience will find valuable—for the purpose of building brand awareness and getting your message across. This is true, and it's a core part of social media.

We'll even go as far as to say that broadcast mode communications are the primary drivers of new growth for digital marketing. Think about it for a moment: Most social media is a "pull" type of marketing (as opposed to "push" type of marketing), You're not able to force people to interact with you; they only come in because you're providing something of value and pulling them in.

Serendipity simply means a happy surprise, or a positive chance occurrence. Have you ever asked people in your networks how they came to find you? We have. And it never ceases to surprise us how people come upon our profiles. Some will find one or another of us after talks we've given, some will find us through organic searches, and some will find us just because a common connection commented on something we put out there. However it happens, we often treat it as a happy accident when someone new decides to come into our networks. But just because it's an accident doesn't mean you can't plan for it. It doesn't mean that you can't do things to encourage this sort of meeting. That is the crux of broadcast mode: putting out good things into the world to set the stage for happy accidents to happen.

Now, although the goal is to develop serendipitous events (and people sharing your content of their own volition), you should still try to measure yourself. There is a relatively predictable pattern that most businesses go through when establishing a new digital marketing broadcast mode plan:

1. Getting set up on a few platforms, and getting started with putting out general messages.
2. After a couple months, the owner doesn't feel that she is getting much traction or results. The proposed solution: add more networks; that'll help![1]
3. A few more months pass, and the business owner is now more overwhelmed than before. Not only is she spending more time on social media than she was before (now that she's managing so many networks), but she's still not getting traction. This is very typical, especially within the first four months or so. The best advice for someone in this situation is to keep with it: it'll work itself out with consistency and stick-to-it-iveness.
4. By about six months, she's getting the hang of it. She's really gotten into the swing of things, and she's starting to see some results. People are beginning to follow the company's account more often, and she's even seeing a few people making product inquiries on her social media sites! All is starting to look up. Re-energized, she doubles her efforts, and really begins to get creative with how she's communicating with her audience in broadcast mode.

---

1   *Remark the authors in a sarcastic tone. It probably won't help.*

5. Reinvigorating her focus really paid off! At the seven-month mark, she's now really starting to see some of her networks take off. Some networks are performing better than others at attracting the types of people she wants to reach and getting the engagement she's looking for. She's also begun to notice, after months of experimenting, what types of updates her audience wants to receive, and which ones get the best engagement results. She's a happy camper, and well on her way to building a profitable social media following.

You may relate in one way or another with the business owner who went through these steps. The fifth step (which people only find by sticking to their editorial calendar and content plan for a while) is one that many business owners and social media managers describe as "finally clicking with my audience."

How to Shout In The Right Direction with Broadcast Mode:

Stick with your editorial calendar and stay consistent as long as you can. Eventually, something will click and you'll find the voice that your audience responds to.

The Campaign Mode

What it is: The "promotion and offering" mode.

What it's good for: Encouraging direct action for an offering that you're promoting.

The key tools for this mode: The SMART goal, action plan.

The goal: A specific business objective; generating leads, closing sales, selling tickets, etc.

How you know if you're successful: Measuring your efforts to meet your goal.

Campaign mode is like broadcast mode, but flipped on its head. In broadcast mode, the most important factor is consistency. In that mode, you might think on any particular day, "I've committed in my editorial calendar to post on Facebook every day. What should I post today?" Campaign mode takes that mentality and turns it upside down. It always starts with a business objective, and uses that objective to drive what messages should go out.

Start with a SMART Goal

In order to have a campaign, you need to have a goal. As we discussed in the first section of the book, having a SMART goals are a great way to get clarity about what you're trying to achieve. By going through the process of outlining your goals, it makes it much simpler to put together an action plan to bring those goals into fruition. Like the old adage says, failing to plan is planning to fail.

These goals can be anything that's relevant to your business at the time. One month you may want to promote a new product offering, and the next month you may want to grow your e-mail list. Whatever the goal is, you can put together a digital marketing campaign to put it into action. But keep in mind that many businesses struggle with following through on an inflated idea of what they can work on all at once. Business owners often tell us, "We're working on all if it," when in truth they may have several half-executed initiatives because they haven't dedicated enough resources to any one of them for it to be successful.

By going through the entire planning process and putting clear and specific SMART goals in place, campaigns can be more effective by focusing your efforts on one or a few goals at once, and thus providing a better chance for success.

By the time you've created your goals for what you would like to carry out, you've already completed half the battle of setting a campaign into motion.

Plan Out the Actions

Now that you know what you want your campaign to do, the next step is to plan out all the actions needed to achieve that goal. These are all the activities that you (and your team, if you have one) will be carrying out over the course of your campaign.

Consider the following simple sample campaign plan:

GOAL: Sell ten tickets to an upcoming class during the month of December.

ACTION PLAN:

1. Create website page with class description and registration information.
2. Record simple video promoting the class to share on YouTube and embed in the website page.
3. Put out three Facebook posts about the class.
4. Tweet four times about the class.
5. Create sample tweets for your referral partners to copy and paste into their Twitter feeds to help you promote the class.
6. Send out one inbox message to contacts on LinkedIn.
7. Post four LinkedIn status updates about the class.
8. Create and share an event listing for the event on Google+.
9. Reference the class in two e-mail newsletters.
10. Send thirty personal e-mails to contacts who would be interested.
11. Send e-mail follow-ups to interested people who have missed previous classes.

By the time that you've created your campaign plan, it should almost be ready to implement itself. A well-created plan doesn't leave any more strategic work to be done later. Now, depending on the stakes of the goal, you may put much more time and effort into evaluating your planned efforts and needed resources. But for a plan with the scope like the one in our example (a small, month-long initiative), the plan need not be overly complex.

How to Shout in the Right Direction with Campaign Mode

Remember your segment, target, position (STP) strategy? If you've gone through that exercise, you will have ended up with a grid diagram that represents all the markets you are going after. To shout in the right direction with campaign mode, focus each campaign to a specific square created from your STP diagram. This will help you make a campaign that is targeted to a particular audience. If you need a refresher, head back to chapter three. To shout in the right direction with campaign mode, focus each campaign to a specific square on your marketing diagram. This will help you make a campaign that is targeted to a particular audience.

The One-to-One Mode

What it is: The "thinking of you" and "personalized service" mode.

What it's good for: Keeping deep relationships with your most valuable contacts.

The key tool for this mode: Your follow-up process.

The goal: Communicate intimately with your close network at scale (with lots of people).

How you know you're successful: You're able to keep in close contact with a large network.

Engaging in one-to-one messages is one of the most overlooked type of actions on social media. Most people are familiar with broadcast mode, and some have even done a campaign in the past. But to even the most experienced social media practitioners and marketers, many don't take the time to do as many one-to-one messages as they could.

The purpose of one-to-one mode is to make people in your network feel important. Like so many facets of social media, one-to-one mode is analogous to connecting and networking in real life. One of the best ways to show one of your friends or networking colleagues that you care about them is to go out of your way to send them a message when you haven't talked in a while. The same can happen on social media. When you go out of your way to make your network feel special, it can deepen your relationship and build lots of good will.

The Power of One-to-One Messages

When Nick first started Tech Nick, one of the first clients he brought on needed a website. Nick's team completed the website, and since the client was fairly tech-savvy, Nick's team was off the hook: the website didn't need any maintenance. As time went on, Nick realized that it had been almost a year since he had talked with this client.

Upon realizing this, Nick sent the client a quick e-mail message asking him how he was doing and if the website was still working well for his company. The response was better than Nick could have expected. The client let Nick know that the website was still working great, but that he had been meaning to get in touch with Nick to introduce him to someone else, who later bought a website. Nick was just doing his customer service due diligence, but ended up getting a solid referral for a new project, all from a one-to-one message.

Start a Conversation

Try using a one-to-one message as an excuse to start up a conversation. Have you seen any news about someone you know that you can talk about? Has one of your contacts put something new on social media that you like? Anything you can think of to start up a conversation can keep your relationship up-to-date.

In particular, communications on social media that are in one-to-one mode have even helped manage time better. As business expands, it's often necessary to cut down on some activities; one common activity that gets cut is networking and "coffee meetings." We've found that as time for those activities goes down, one-to-one communications over social media can help you keep in touch with a large network of people, even if you don't see them in person as often.

Put Together a Plan

What would happen if you made one-to-one messaging a part of your normal process for customers? A lot of good things, that's what would happen. Your customers would know that you care about them, they would know that you understand what is going on in their world, and they would know that your business has it together enough to remember to keep in touch.

There are lots of different ways to make one-to-one messaging a part of your normal operating plan. Sometimes these messages can be over e-mail, and other times they can be a tweet, Facebook wall post, or LinkedIn message. They can be a mention on an Instagram picture or even a review on Google+.

The most important thing is to add some reliable reminder to go out and do these unsolicited activities as often as you can.

One-to-One Social Media Actions Aren't Just for Marketing

Consider Comcast Cable, the nation's largest cable, high-speed Internet, and phone provider to residential customers. We interviewed the manager for social media and learned how he and his team used their social media. Around 2007, Comcast started engaging with customers using social media on a very small scale, specifically to offer a new channel for customer support. After seeing the amount of people complaining on social media, they thought, "Why should we force our customers to use the phone when they need help?" They found this out simply by reading all of the comments they received on Twitter and Facebook. This became two opportunities for Comcast: first, to adapt to the shifting way customers were dealing with frustrations and support, and secondly, to monitor what their customers are thinking.

People will vent their feelings about a business now on social media and direct it towards the business. If a business isn't available to acknowledge, if not fix the problem, it becomes a lost opportunity and remains a negative experience for the customer, even if the customer wasn't seeking help. Comcast used this opportunity to transform a negative situation into a positive one, or at least into a less negative one. When this happens, businesses create stronger customer bonds.

Small businesses can adopt this strategy, too. In most cases, a small business can avoid corporate filters and naturally be more personal. The volume of social media support is significantly smaller, too. If your business doesn't receive many inbound support requests, this may not be an option for you.

How to Shout in the Right Direction with One-to-One Mode

Don't do one-to-one mode communications only for sales and prospects. It may be tempting to use social media to prod your prospects down the sales pipeline (which you can do), but don't use one-to-one mode only for sales. People will think better of you if you reach out to them both when there's a sale on the table and when there isn't.

22

Building a Following

It seems like the central tenant of social media marketing is to "build a following." Build a following, build a following, build a following. That's all anyone talks about! While it's certainly an important task, it's not something that just happens on its own. Building a following is one of the core tasks of social media strategy: it's one of the things it does best. A powerful community can make or break a brand by acting as advocates, driving promotion efforts, and helping spread the word about your company. But how, exactly, does one go about building a community of real value? That is where you come in.

What, Exactly, Makes Content Good?

The core of any good online customer relationship is based on one thing: value. For the most part, the best online marketing centers around providing potential customers with something they want. And by value, we mean value in the broadest sense. Whether you're trying to figure out what type of blog article to write, what type of e-mail to send, or what type of Facebook update to post, you'll build the best communities when you focus on giving customers value.

This is where the fun part comes in. How you plan to create value for your community is the crux of your plan's success. It's one thing to decide that you're going to set up shop on Facebook, but it's quite another to come up with the content to post and manage a thriving community. The content that you put out should reflect your understanding of the type of value people want to get out of their online interactions with you. And the benefits range widely.

Some of the ways you can provide value are:
- Sharing your advice, knowledge, and tips.
- Giving previews and discounts for your service or product.
- Connecting users with others whom they might like to know.
- Giving customers a vision for the future (this is a key value driver for Pinterest, for example).
- Providing an interesting or funny media experience; things like photographs, video, etc.
- Letting customers know your company and staff better: having that human connection is a value in and of itself.

As you might imagine, there are as many different ways to create value as the day is long. The biggest part of defining your company's strategy is finding out what path to creating value is best for your marketing and your audience. Even better, the way that you go about creating value should resonate with the segments of customers you're trying to attract (that is why you made the segments, isn't it?).

Either Train Yourself to Be Creative, or Find Creative People to Help (or Both)

We often see digital marketing initiatives at companies fail because the people running them don't plan for the sheer amount of creative effort that goes into putting out content that makes real connections. The same people often don't consider themselves as "creative people," and use that attitude as an obstacle to their success in implementing a marketing plan that works. Furthermore, after admitting that they don't want to be involved in a heavily creative pursuit, they don't bring on creative people to help them.

Being creative is the key to succeeding in social media. If you want your strategy to work, you're going to either have to become creative, or hire someone who is. And you have to like it! If you have to force yourself to write a blog article, customers will smell your distaste from a mile way. Similarly, if you're passionate about the creative process, that will seep through in your messages as well.

If you're a delegator who decides to bring on creative help, remember: these people are artists. Whether this person you bring on is a social media manager, blogger, marketer, web developer, copywriter, graphic designer, or other creative worker, he or she is your creator, even though that person may also be your vendor. Yes, you're paying your creative people and you should reasonably expect that they perform, but we can't tell you how much of a difference it makes to see your creative workers as artists. The same designer can put out crap and brilliance for the same fee, so it behooves you as a businessperson to help him or her cultivate that artistic feel when working on behalf of your brand. A little creative appreciation can go a long way.

If You've Got a Good Idea, You Shouldn't Have to Sell It Hard

Most of us in business and marketing are natural persuaders. The compliment "she could sell ice to Eskimos" isn't often conferred lightly, and those of us who are drawn to the business of influence are often great at doing it. There are cases, though, where having the ability to "sell anything" can get in the way. In some ways, if your idea is good enough, it shouldn't have to be pushed. If it really, truly hits on what your customers want, you shouldn't have to turn the sales and marketing strong arm on overdrive to cram it down peoples' throats.

This is where learning to shout in the right direction becomes important. If your product or service sales aren't up to your expectations, you can analyze several factors about your marketing, targeting, or promotion to improve. You may not be positioning your product well, or maybe you offer a product that people don't *actually* want. Or maybe the product has potential, but you're promoting it to the wrong audience. Whatever the case, being sensitive to how hard you're working to promote your product will indicate whether you need to improve something in the marketing strategy to establish a better fit.

Many business owners report refining their offerings and target markets again and again until they finally feel that their strategy is clicking. What you're doing clicks when an offering that you used to have to promote at full strength begins to bring in customers on its own. When you begin to be surprised at how far referrals travel through your network, you'll get some evidence that you've found the right fit between customer and product or service.

Build Up Your Social Currency

We're big fans of "social currency," a concept described notably in Scott Stratten's book *UnMarketing* (among other places). Businesses using social media often have a hard time *actually* generating sales or other valuable action from social media activities. In this pursuit of driving action, they sometimes try to use their social media profiles like television ads; shoving marketing messages down the throats of their community members. Such an approach misses the point and the ethos of how to connect over social media.

Nothing on the web works in this way. People aren't as receptive to social media sales messages as they are to sales messages on traditional media: that is, not unless they're earned.

You definitely can promote your business and make sales with social media, but the ability to do so doesn't come freely: in fact, it can sometimes be quite expensive. The cost, though, is not in dollars, but social currency. In order to earn the right to ask your community to do something for you (e.g., share your message, buy your product, comment, etc.) you must have first done something for them. The more you give to your community by providing them value, the more social currency you build up into your "bank account" to earn the right to ask favors.

Viewed in this light, you will find that it most certainly is okay to ask for sales on social media, but only as much as you've helped your community.

23

How to Develop Amazing Messages

What does it mean to make a message? At its core, businesses send many, many messages to their customers—often many more than they're aware of. Every time your brand enters a customer's life, you send a message. Everything—from the first time they hear someone mention your name, to their first visit to your website, to the first time you pick up the phone when they call—sends a message.

Any time you have a chance to influence your audience, from the very first touch to the very last, you'll want to make sure that your brand comes across as clearly as possible.

Making that magic message is a central piece to shouting in the right direction. That magic message happens when you combine an in-depth understanding of who your perfect customers are with an awesome promotion and communication plan to get it into their hands. In this section, we discuss some of the principles of making that magic happen.

Simplicity

Few have described a better approach to simplicity than Albert Einstein, who famously said, "Things should be made as simple as possible, but no simpler." The same is true for creating your marketing messages. Especially in today's attention-starved Internet culture, every second of mind time that a customer devotes to your brand is one to treasure. And only a simple approach can reach people in just one second.

In nearly every case, simpler is better. Simplicity forces us to condense our message down to its core, rejecting all the rest.

Take a company website, for example. For a website to be effective, it must encourage people to take one of a limited number of actions. Most web analytics data shows that the more options you provide users, the less they take advantage of any of the options. In the early days of content management systems running websites, webmasters got so drunk on the power of easily being able to add pages that they packed websites with pages out the wazoo. At the time, designers made faux pas that today's more minimalist professionals would have scoffed at; things like having huge drop-down menus, extraneous photo galleries, and over-stuffed text on pages. In this case, removing unnecessary features like these helps direct users to more important actions by making calls to action easier to find and comprehend.

The same is true for every message you put out. For example, have you tried to introduce yourself at a professional networking event recently? What is it like to explain you and your company to new people? Do they understand easily? If not, are there any pieces of your pitch that you can remove to help with clarity? This is the type of iterative process that you can go through to make your message simpler and easier to understand.

That being said, there is a *huge* difference between "simple" and "easy." As you may have found before, creating a simple message to describe your company or pitch a service can be anything but easy. It can even be painful for some business owners to have to go through their messages and cut things that they feel attached to, or that they *think* they need to get across. In the web design business, for example, we're often tasked with the tough job of convincing owners of companies to relinquish their hold on pages that aren't directly contributing to the communication of their core message. Predictably, the process is often painful for all, as it calls into question the "importance" of pieces of content that took time for someone to develop. But, also predictably, after going through the process, the improved website has everyone happy by the time the improvements are over.

This is the power of simplicity. Embrace it, and it has the power to make your messages more compelling and effective.

Cut. Cut Some More. Then Cut Even More

One of the easiest ways to embrace simplicity in your communications is to cut content. In general, we've found that marketers often fall in the trap of saying, "I know so much about this; if I tell people more, they'll buy more because they'll realize that I know so much."

It doesn't work that way. Odds are, your message may have more content than you need to successfully get your message across.

Take the example of a small business website again. The average small business website goes through an evolution in the amount and quality of content that the website contains.[1]

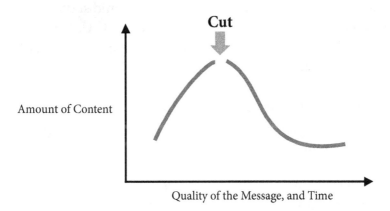

1   *This is, of course, based on no actual study outside of our general experience.*

This is because when messages first evolve, only a small amount of content is written; and the content that is written hasn't had the benefit of experience (so to speak). As time goes on, the creators develop more and more content in an effort to boost the message. It's not necessarily better content overall, just more content.

The best messaging comes from taking that "hump" and cutting it WAY down. Not only will you likely end up with less content and text than you began with, but you also will have distilled the message down to the absolute most effective chunks. That's the power of cutting. Over time, you end up with the very best.

Isn't that a good way to respect your customers' time? We've all heard about the short attention spans of today's online consumer: they're short. When you cut down your message, you're making sure to fill customers' limited attention with only the best.

Beware of the Curse of Knowledge

Marketers (not being immune to the cognitive biases that plague all humans) are subject to a bias known as "the curse of knowledge," which makes it difficult for well-informed people to fully understand lesser-informed people.

This poses a particular challenge when crafting a message: You are the most well-informed person about your products and services, and your job is to educate and convince the less-informed. Unfortunately, the curse of knowledge may bias you against understanding the very people you need to understand most!

When preparing your message, take into account your own blindness when it comes to understanding your customers: Go out and talk to them as much as possible.

In Steven Gary Blank's book Four Steps to the Epiphany, he astutely observes, "No facts exist inside the building, only opinions." This is compounded by the curse of knowledge, making us as marketers much worse than we think at predicting what customers want. The only way to know for sure (and, it follows, to shout in the right direction by developing a message that your target customers care about) is to go out and talk with them.

Messages Aren't Just Text; They're Visual

Unfortunately, having the right content is only half the battle. Even the most expertly written copy can be obscured by other components of visual communication. For example, a message's font choice can affect how the message is perceived, how it's read, and what emotions people associate with it. And we haven't even gotten into the positioning, layout, color, calls to action, and a zillion other design factors.

As your putting your messages into practice, remember that what you say is not the be-all and end-all. Just as nonverbal factors determine a significant amount of how verbal communication is perceived, design elements dictate a similar amount about written communication.

Take Advantage of Emotional First Impressions

When you're designing the layout of your message, take special account of the order in which you convey information. People make decisions with their emotional minds first, then use their rational minds to justify the decision. To compound this effect, people are also unaware that they do this, according to psychologists. This effect also leads to *confirmation bias*, which causes people to seek out information that validates their already-held beliefs.

As a marketer, this means that the first impression you give your audience is extremely important, given how much the first impression can affect and even override later logical decision making.

This means that your brand's initial visual impression gets conveyed nearly instantly and has a huge effect on the customer's perception of you. This impression is largely emotional and visual, which implies some specific design practices for you as you design "first impression":

1. Use more graphics than text to communicate emotion.
2. Emphasize emotional messages over logical arguments.
3. Drill down to your market's overarching needs and concerns to craft an emotional message.

In a website design scenario, the first impression area may be the home page. If so, the rest of the site can describe the services in detail, using copy that's designed to satisfy the logical mind and strengthen any impulsive decision the visitor has already unconsciously made.

Saying No to Good Ideas

Anyone who spends even a small amount of time in marketing, sales, or digital strategy usually doesn't have trouble identifying different strategies that are available to them. Often, marketing plans are filled with huge lists of actions, strategies, approaches, platforms, and so on. While this is a fantastic first step, we find that most companies (especially small companies without a dedicated marketing person) are usually *more* limited by the time they have to devote to each of the available strategies than they are in their understanding of the different strategies that are out there to take advantage of.

Take the simple example of just choosing which social media platforms to participate in. While it may be true that any of the social networks can provide value to your marketing plan, your company may not have the resources to pay someone to manage all of them. So deciding to hire someone is more pressing then deciding to learn about all of those social media networks.

A large part of having a great message is developing shrewd priorities, and being able to say "no" to good ideas that may very well provide business value so that other more manageable and perhaps more promising (in the short-term!) ideas can survive.

24

Pay Attention to Details

As business people, we all have a different idea of how it feels to use our products than our customers have. To make matters worse, each customer experiences the product differently from any other. So it's important to give special attention to customer experience. How do customers feel at every point during their interaction with you? Make a list of every action the customer needs to take to do business with you, including activities in your sales process, the quoting process, the negotiation to fulfillment, the follow-up, and every step in between. Every one of these interactions is an opportunity for creativity in wowing the customer.

At some levels, this means being true to your brand identity.

The amount of detail you pay attention to may vary, depending on your level of technological knowledge. The amount of detail that you customize may increase as you learn more about the system you're using.

Always Make Your Touchpoints Better

- Your website home page
- Your e-mail list
- Your Facebook page
- Your blog
- The voice you use
- How easy it is to contact you
- The visual look and feel of ALL your elements (including things you didn't have designed)

Paying attention to details can yield practical benefits. Here's an example of a few changes you might make to your website's contact page that can improve customer experience.

1. A website has a static contact page with an e-mail address.
2. That page may be improved by adding your business's phone number, address, and map to accommodate more contact methods.
3. That page may be improved by adding a contact form.
4. That contact form may be improved by adding a return message to the user, indicating that the message was received.
5. That message may be improved by rewriting the default message to make sure it matches brand identity and business goals.

Detail Your Brand Feeling

What do you want people to think and feel when they hear the name of your company for the first time? This should be intentional. Whether you're putting your brand name or other kind of message out there, being intentional about how you want people to feel will increase the impact of the message.

Be aware that your customers' feeling may change over the cycle in which they interact with you. That cycle includes:

1. Awareness
2. Learning about your offerings
3. Sales process (if applicable)
4. Purchase
5. Fulfillment
6. Completion (if applicable)
7. Follow-up

At each point in the process, you will want to define both how customers often feel at that stage and how you *want* them to feel at that stage (if those two are different). So write down each step in the process above that's relevant to your interactions with customers and define how your customers are likely feeling and how you want them to feel at that stage. Then consider how you might bring the two into greater alignment, including through creative ways of getting your messages across.

Relate Messages to Specific Audiences

We often see marketers begin the creative process with *what they have to offer* instead *of what their core customer wants to buy.* The art of creating a creative message that shouts in the right direction starts with considering a specific customer. When you are ruthless about delivering what your specific customer wants without being burdened by what you have to offer, your creative output will be much better because of it.

Are You Ready to Change Direction if You Need to?

How can you learn that your customers use your offering in a way you didn't intend? And how can capitalize on the fact that this happens, probably more than you know?

People tend to like to be told how to use something, as it creates less cognitive dissonance. If one of your customers, however, has gone to enough length to adapt your product or service to meet one of their needs, you know that the need is very strong. If you find multiple people doing the same thing independently, it's about time to adjust your offering and your message to incorporate this "off-label" use.

25

Show a Path to Satisfaction in Your Marketing by Giving Customers Their "Moments"

Sometimes, the best messages come out of little details. Whether you're coming up with a Facebook post, website copy, e-mail newsletter content, or any other type of message, there is lots of power that comes with being specific. Some of the most effective messaging comes from resonating directly with users. After all, they want to know that you understand what it's like to be in their shoes.

To *really* resonate with your customers, you have to be aware of what it's like to be them at every step of your business process. Then, and only then, can you create messages that truly hit home. To do this, take some time to consider aspects of your customer's experience that impact how they ultimately feel about your product. Do some brainstorming. Pull out your product and try it yourself, or have someone on your team perform your service to you. We promise: Discovering what your customers experience will be enlightening. For each of the "moments" below, consider your customers and business model to describe situations that would cause your customers to think that way.

The "My Current Solution Isn't Working" Moment

In this moment, something about your customers' lives makes them realize that what they're doing, including using your product or service, isn't working. Do they conclude this in a single moment of revelation? Is it due to a build-up of little irritations? Did a question from a friend or colleague make them reconsider the choices they've made?

Whatever it is, most customers go through a moment like this, one that causes them to question what they are doing and motivates them to find another solution like yours.

The "So, I Don't Have to Rearrange My Life to Use This" Moment

Once someone opens up his or her mind to the possibility of even considering your company, one of the first thoughts that arises is "How much work is this going to be?" This is especially true for business-to-business situations, since businesses often must change how they work to incorporate new offerings. It's not just businesses that think this way, though; consumers also worry about how much work it will take to incorporate a new product into their lives.

To combat that, if your product is easy to purchase and incorporate in the customer's way of life, getting them to realize that is a great goal to have. Make sure that your education process highlights what it's like to begin using your product or service. Let customers know how easy it can be, and that you'll be there to help them at every step of the way.

The "I Wasn't Expecting This to Be So Fun" Moment

Have you ever tried a product or service that performed exactly as you expected it to perform? We have. And when things perform as expected, we're satisfied, but that's about it; we don't typically end up forming any negative feelings about it, but we also don't form any awesomely great ones, either.

While this isn't bad, it's not exactly the recipe for great marketing. Great marketing builds in moments of exceeding expectations to make sure customers know that they're getting more value than they expected.

What about your product or service can surprise a customer, causing them to have fun using it? Just because you may be solving a boring problem doesn't mean that your solution needs to be boring![1] If there is anything about your solutions or process that will be fun for the customer, let them know about it in advance in your marketing. It will help them make an easier decision knowing that good emotions are in store for them if they choose you.

The "Hmm, This Really Does Work" moment

Whatever your product or service is, your marketing makes promises and sets expectations about what the customer's experience will be. When you set up expectations like this, customers are continuously judging whether or not the delivered experience meets what they expected.

Some of the best products and services open customers' eyes to possibilities they didn't previously know existed. Find out what parts of your product or service offer surprising new possibilities to your clients, and make sure they have their moment.

The "I Can't Believe That I Never Have to Deal With THAT Anymore" Moment

Giving your customers a moment like this can be an amazing way to generate loyalty. If you have a product or service whose benefit is pain relief of some kind, creating a moment like this is essential.

When people sign up for a service or purchase a product to help them avoid a pain or frustration (and it doesn't have to be a physical pain), they often go through a period of skepticism. But if what you offer meets their needs, using your product successfully may give customers a sud-

---

1   *We've also seen some companies suck ALL the fun out of services that are supposed to be fun. Look out for that, too.*

den realization that the pain they purchased your product or service to avoid is really, truly gone. This is nirvana for both them and you.

Take some time to figure out what those pain-relief moments are for your customers. Knowing this can help you to create really great marketing messages, showing potential customers the path to pain relief that other customers already experience.

The "My Boss/Coworker/Wife/Husband/Friend Recognizes That I Made a Good Decision" Moment

When a customer makes a decision to buy your product, remember that their decision doesn't happen in a bubble. They may have been the decision maker for the purchase, but there are many others in the customer's life who have an impact on whether the customer ultimately reaches consensus as to if they've made a savvy purchase or not.

These people in their network, their boss, co-workers, significant others, etc., might inquire about their purchase with you to make sure they didn't get taken by you. And they can't help it! Typically they've got the customer's best interests in mind, but the approval of those close to the customer plays a huge role in the customer's satisfaction with their purchase from you.

If all goes well, those close to the customer will reinforce their decision to buy from you. This is good for all around, because you have helped the customer gain something above and beyond what deliverables you promised: the approval of peers. The customer stuck their neck out making a purchase, and you didn't burn them for it. Good for you.

This also can go the other way. If a customer buys from you, their personal pride is wrapped up in saving face for having spent money with you. If you don't deliver, or if others in the customer's network come to the impression the customer didn't spend their money wisely with you, this can do even more damage than we often realize.

Answering these questions will help you discover your customers' specific routes to satisfaction, and help you find a way to convey the potential for satisfaction to others who have not yet purchased.

So poll your customers and do some research. Once you have some answers, design a campaign to center around this. Naïve customers[2] who are coming in contact with your message for the first time will appreciate having concrete, bite-sized messages that are about the tangible payoffs of being your customers.

2   *These are customers who haven't heard about your company before, not customers who are naïve themselves.*

26

Conclusion: How to Turn All This into Action

Whew. We have gone over a lot together. We've discussed powerful strategies and practical ideas to help you grow your business by shouting in the right direction. But now we're at the end of the line. As our childhood hero, Smokey Bear, always said, "Only you can prevent forest fires." The main point of his mantra isn't just about fighting fires, but about helping everyone recognize how important their individual contributions and efforts are to progressing a larger goal. The goal of the book has been to provide a series of actionable strategies that you can deploy in your business immediately. In order to get the value out of the book that you and your business deserve, don't wait to put some of these ideas into practice. Ideas are useless when they're locked inside your brain. Even if you take just one of these ideas and put it to use immediately, you will have wisely invested twenty bucks and a weekend into reading this book.

Why is it so hard to change? Why is it so hard to implement new ideas? We, as representatives of the humble human race, are hard-coded creatures of habit. We all (especially business folk) attempt to make habits to help us make sense of our day-to-day lives and get where we want to be.

Though this can be a good thing when habits helps us make consistent progress toward our objectives, habits also can be powerful supporters of the status quo and key drivers of resistance to change.

Why is it so hard to change? Why is it so hard to implement new ideas? We, as representatives of the humble human race, are hard-coded creatures of habit. We all (especially business folk) attempt to make habits to help us make sense of our day-to-day lives and get where we want to be. Though this can be a good thing when habits helps us make consistent progress toward our objectives, habits also can be powerful supporters of the status quo and key drivers of resistance to change.

Your mission as the ambassador of change is to embrace uncertainty for your business. This is no small order. When you invite change into your business, many things will likely have to shift. And everyone and everything—from employees to branding—need to be ready, able, and willing to take the associated risks, if only little ones, to reach new goals. If you really want to change, and you really want to make it happen, this is your moment of truth.

How does this start? It is nothing like flipping a switch or simply saying that you will do a little bit more of this and a little bit more of that. Yes, small changes made over a long period of time can have long-term impact, but to what purpose? To what goal? Taking advantage of change involves a top-to-bottom look at your business.

The first step is to create a plan. It doesn't matter how small or big the plan is. As long as you have something down on paper to explain the who, what, where, when, how, and—of course—the why, you have a plan. If you don't quite have a thorough why, consider these as inspiration:

- To turn the business around
- To start a new venture
- To launch a new product
- To hit your revenue targets
- To get creative
- To build a following

- To share your knowledge
- To make a difference

Don't let us convince you to do something that you don't want to do—or worse, can't do effectively. The worst that can happen is that you create a plan that that you can't execute. This can occur when you build a mountain out of the perfect plan and can't get up the will, strength, or know-how to carry it out. It's like an amateur attempting to climb K2 or Mount Everest. She sits at the bottom, staring at the top, "getting ready to get ready," waiting for the day when she's prepared to climb. In other words, done is better than perfect. And when you execute even a small plan, you're done.

To create successful plan, go through what you've come up with to implement it. Are there activities you need to cut? Are you excited about everything you've committed yourself to do? When can you get them done by? Everything on your implementation plan must be given one of the following statuses:

1. Put it into action immediately.
2. Table it until a documented date for revisiting.
3. Admit to yourself that you're not actually committed to doing it.

As we noted earlier, it is okay to cut things from your plan. Actually, it feels pretty good when you have one less thing to do. Then springboard off this feeling to get started on the rest. One of the most powerful inhibitors of putting plans to action is the business owner's delusion that she can have a million goals that all have high priority.

Steven Covey, in *7 Habits of Highly Effective People*, says, "Begin with the end in mind." One of the beauties of strategic planning is that you can use it to get anywhere: You just have to decide where you want to go. You can make your plan as audacious as you please: but you have to have a vision. And if you want to accomplish it, you need to gather the necessary resources and commit 100 percent.

If there are three, absolute and fundamental pieces of advice we can leave you to shout in the right direction, it's these:

Make a plan that is both actionable and aligned with business goals.
Choose the tools that arm your plan to connect with your audience.
Develop creative messages that tell a compelling story.

As you go forward with your plan and business, remember to shout in the right direction. Using the tools of strategic planning and focus in this book, you will be able to make your mark on the world by getting your message across to exactly the right people.

#ShoutBook

Acknowledgements

Special thanks to:

Comcast Cable
Davis Law Office
DipYourCar
LASER Classroom
Mayo Clinic
tena.cious social + design

Your perspectives and experiences helped bring one of our favorite topics to life. Thank you.

About The Authors

Eric Lehnen, Co-author

Eric is marketing tactician. Creating the perfect plan to overcome business problems is his version of crack. 9-5, he is a marketing specialist at a software company, but at home he is an entrepreneur. He has helped start a nightclub, advertising agency and a mobile app company while consulting others on the side. Outside of marketing, Eric loves philosophy, technology and traveling.
Twitter: @ericlehnen

Nick Rosener, CSMS, Co-Author

Nick is the owner of Tech Nick Creative, a web marketing company in Minneapolis, MN. At night, he dreams about social media, web design, blog strategy, and other ways to help small and medium companies grow using the web. Nick is a speaker and instructor on social media strategy, teaching a course on the topic at Century College, Argosy University, and North Hennepin Community College.
Twitter: @nickrosener

Speaking Engagements

Help your organization shout in the right direction.

Shout In the Right Direction is more than just a book, it's a practical approach for improving the marketing at your organization. The keynote speeches and workshops described below are ideal complements to a conference or meeting of business owners or marketing professionals.

Keynote:

A 45- or 60-minute presentation covering essentials of segmenting and targeting. Participants will:

- Get excited about understanding customers more deeply.
- Empower themselves to focus resources effectively.
- Walk away with the basic tools to frame up their marketing plan.

Workshop:

An hour-long, half-day, or full-day interactive marketing strategy workshop, where participants will:

- Outline segments, targets, and positioning for their own company.
- Understand Social Media Actions and how to leverage them to reach customers.
- Develop a plan to align social media with strategic business goals.

For more information on Keynote and Workshop availability and fees, contact the authors at www.shoutintherightdirection.com.

www.ingramcontent.com/pod-product-compliance
Lightning Source LLC
Chambersburg PA
CBHW070947050326
40689CB00014B/3373